ACKNOWLEDGEMENTS

I think that the pause to consider all who have helped forge this book is among the most humbling experiences which has befallen me. Names not recalled of teachers who taught me and forced writing from me; authors and mentors who forced me to think; friends and those who shaped me in their passing on their journeys; those who fed me, lent me a place to lay my head, gave me their ancestry and their history—are they all not the pages that build the book.

But there are those pages—those pages whose sparkle we remember, those whose images made us stop, lean back and smile with remembrance and respect. And it is these I would bring to you with gratitude:

Dr. Bill Gothard, who first and consistently challenged me to meditate on God's Word, and when I did, gave me the opportunity to tell of its wonders;

Dr. Laurel Briscoe, for his prayers and for his excellent editing and critique of my "writing" and "punctuation";

Terry A. Anderson, for his life of telling others of a relationship with God, our Father, and God's use of his life to supply that message to so many;

My mother, Marlene Davis, saint, angel, warrior; prayed me into the kingdom and prayed this book into existence (you are deeply loved); my father, Duane Davis, for giving me a Godly heritage, and for showing me what it was to stand for what is right; my other mother, Peggy Sparks, for praying for us everyday for years—the borders are increased; Jim Sparks, for his prayers, wisdom, and support.

The many prayers Dick Bertram, of the students of the International Ministerial Institute, and the Board of Directors of Alive, Inc. Gordon Bergstrom, and Les and Betty Daniels; Bobby Horton, thanks for the Stonewall eyes and all the music for the battle;

And finally my life partner in the battle, my love and my wife, my Mary, for all the truth shared, for the communion of pain, the unity of the path of the kingdom and death to self and life to our King. (And help with the Appendices.)

And to Him who is able to keep you from stumbling, and to make you stand in the presence of His glory blameless with great joy, to Yahweh, our God and Father, who saved me from myself through His Son, Yeshua, and keeps me in His Spirit.

Your Face, Oh Lord, I Shall Seek

Michael Davis

NEW LIFE PUBLISHING, INC.
P. O. BOX 747
BURNET, TEXAS 78611

All Scripture, unless otherwise noted is quoted from the
New American Standard Bible, Copyright © 1960, 1962, 1963,
1968, 1971, 1972, 1973, 1975, 1977, 1995 by the
Lockman Foundation. Used by permission.

ISBN 978-0-615-53123-6

CONTENTS

PREFACE

I thought seriously about naming this preface, "Reasons why you will hate this book." This book is about having a relationship with God and seemingly should not be hated. The contents are true enough, and not that poorly written. The points, I believe, are proven Biblically. But let us own up to it, you and I are basically lazy and self seeking. For someone to come along and say that a relationship with God may require something on my part other than attending religious services, giving money, or the occasional condescension on my part to give some time is a bit much. We have come to believe, because it has been taught to us (or at least strongly insinuated) by our religious leaders that we are so special that God is just excited for us to sit and listen to them talk about God. We pay the pastor, priest, rabbi to know God for me. That has become our relationship to God. Would you define that as relationship? Can our current (and past) religious systems be what God means when He says, "Seek My face"?

Another personally irritating issue and as discussed in these chapters, is that the Bible is full of conditional promises; "If-then" statements. I want those promises without responsibility on my part. I want a relationship that costs me nothing. I want God's blessings on my life without His holiness in my life. God's economy does not work that way. Period.

Most of us are not desperate for a relationship with our Heavenly Father; religion will do just fine. Real effort to seek Him is not what I have been taught or desire. I am more in despair than desperate.

This is not a book to tell you that you should have a relationship with God (you should); or how amazing a relationship with Him is (it is); but rather <u>how</u> to have a relationship with Him. This book is about work, and as such, will not be one of those inspirational books that gets one worked up into a frenzy to rush after the latest fad. That said, it is also not about "works" for salvation; it is about the work that any relationship requires, in this case a relationship with the God of the universe.

And it is not easy. Work may be enjoyable at times, but it is rarely easy—that is why it is work. Yes, God's grace is there for us. But it is we who have made relationship hard. God says over and over that it our sin, iniquity, and transgression have separated us from Him. Through Messiah He has offered the perfect answer to those impediments to relationship with Him. But we do continue to insist on our ways rather than His, and thereby again separate ourselves from His life. We have cheapened and wrongly defined grace, making it a magic word which has God agreeing with whatever I want. Could you enjoy or sustain a relationship with a person who would put on you the same self-centered demands we put on God?

And relationship is not fast. Everything in our society is about being fast. I need my gratification now; I must hurry off to the next thing; peace is not lasting; happiness is fleeting; love is temporary. God's ways are endurance, patience, waiting, planting, reaping, sowing. The contents of this book shed light from God's Word on troubled areas of our lives. Contained in these pages are the answers. My, that sounds rather arrogant doesn't it? But the words of this book do not rest on the promises and ways of man; we are only quoting and displaying God's answers. He is the way. He is your answer. I being human will believe lies, and then live them out or pass them on to others. We all have believed and still believe things about God that are not true.

No, you and your denomination do not hold all truth. That is God's jurisdiction and responsibility.

The invitation is not to follow me or anyone else. <u>You</u> are to know God personally. <u>You</u> are to follow Christ personally. I do not want your money or your loyalty. I do not want you to like me. People that want to be popular and well liked lose their lives to the popularity; they are owned by others. All of us really need to be owned by God through Jesus, our Lord. Life is not found in relationship with others of our kind; life is not found in any religion. Life, and it eternal is found in relationship with God, being "one" with Him. When He is living in me—God and I are one being—it is impossible for me to die. Jesus (Yeshua, Messiah) said in John 17:3, "This is eternal life, that they may know You, the only true God, and Jesus Christ whom You have sent." Eternal life is knowing God and His Son—intimately.

Psalm 27:8

> When You said, "Seek My face,"
> my heart said to You,
> "Your face, O Lord, I shall seek."

Chapter 1
The Bomb Will Drop

Ecclesiastes 12:12 states, "The writing of many books is endless." I can tell you the writing of just one seems endless! And I have so hesitated to add another book to the Christian collection when we are in an age in which The Book is far too often ignored or discounted. I have been pushed (encouraged) by lovers of The Book because the purpose of this book is to decrease that The Other may increase.

This book is not written by one who has it "all together" or has arrived. In fact, it has been written because I am a failure. Knowing and accepting that fact is really quite freeing. It is those that are failures and know it, that reach for The One That Never Fails. Jesus never said "narrow is the place" when you have arrived; He said, "...narrow is the way." Which is really what, I believe He wants from us—to be on "the way" in Him. God is not concerned about our social or religious position or appearance or our togetherness. The Beatitudes do not start or end with "blessed are the together..."

As I have watched the crumbling of our nation and world, with the acceptance and legalization of evil and perversion and the scattering of families as our society has replaced the fruit of responsible parenthood with the harvest of hedonism; and as I have noted the self-centered lies on which these maledictions base in light of the sacrificial truths of the Bible, I would wonder how we got to this point. I wanted to know who had compromised, who lacked vigilance on their watch, to find the point of that error and repair the breach. My investigation has time and time again clearly pointed to the place where the choices have consistently been self over others, lust over love, and has brought heartache to family, compromise to Christianity, license to law, excuses to responsibility—the breach is *me*. I do not mean I am the center of evil in the universe, but I am a sinner of evil in the universe, and my leaven permeates much. But, just as I cannot be blamed for all that is evil, neither can I blame another for my evil. Humorist Walt Kelly stated it as, "We have met the enemy and he is us." Jesus Christ stated it with his every breath; for the key to revival in our churches and country is not programs or money or people—it is always "*me*". Jesus did not say, "Blessed are all those other people if they would just start being poor in spirit." He did not say I was responsible to make them be pure in heart, hungry for righteousness, willing to suffer for righteousness. He instead said I am responsible for those qualities in me. In Matthew 7:5 Jesus gives us the key to effective ministry: "You hypocrite, first take the log out of your own eye, and then you will see clearly to take the speck out of your brother's eye." I must first understand my own hypocrisy. Jesus' words, "You hypocrite" are in the present tense. They ring true for me now and will always ring true. One of the first steps to entering the kingdom of God is to agree always with the King. There are few epithets lower than hypocrite, but the more I accept Jesus' assessment of me, the freer I become from my pride, ambitions, and me. Jesus' next statement lets us know how to help those poor afflicted souls with all those "specks' in their eyes that bother me so: "first take the log out of your own eye and then you will see clearly to take the speck out of your brother's eye." He tells us there is a way to help others, but it begins with me, and dealing with my sin and my self-centeredness and my self-righteousness. Jesus' words from Matthew 6 put in the first person state it another way, " I am the salt of the

earth, but if I have lost my saltiness I am good for nothing…"
In my life the problem is *me*. In your life the problem is you.

Now I certainly have not always believed such things.
Until recently, the whole truth and nothing but the truth, was
of very little concern to me. I mean, the truth was okay, but it
did not apply to me. I was busy! Busy working for God!
Busy fixing people! (They never stayed fixed—neither did
God.) I was a deacon in our church! My wife and I lead and
trained counseling and prayer teams! When the church
doors were open we were there! If we weren't attending a
meeting, there were always meetings! And if not that,
meetings could be found! There was always something to
which to say "Yes!" We were living the life of the American
church! We were busy! If I ever stopped long enough to
determine if there was any real fruit in my life I don't
remember. (I was far too busy producing the fruit of "busy-
ness"). I had no idea how God defined fruit anyway, and
was far too busy working for Him to stop to talk to Him about
that or any other subject.

Of course, there were some problems in my
pretentious paradise. I did seem to have some ongoing
problems with anger. And I did sort of have a cold heart
toward my wife, and children, and friends…and the
church…and the lost…and God. And I was never very
loving or kind. And sometimes my mouth did say very hurtful
things to others. And while I read about joy in Scripture and
that I was supposed to have it, it was non-existent in my life.
Oh, and sin seemed to have a lot of control in my life. But
that at least was consistent with my lack of self-control.
While I appeared successful on the outside, I knew that
every area of my life was actually fraught with failure and
disappointment. You can image that with this list there may
have been a few other little problems here and there. But

one that was increasingly difficult to ignore was my cold heart toward Jesus and my total lack of relationship with Him.

I, like most, had come to equate working for God with abiding in God and loving God. Scripture, of course, never equates these two, but, as I did not spend much time in Scripture, that could not have bothered me much. Since I was so busy working for God, I knew I <u>must</u> be abiding in Him and, therefore, must also be "walking by the spirit" (whatever that meant); and, therefore, I was certainly being led by God! Again, I never stopped to question what I was doing, whether it was right, what was really being done, or if it truly was what God said would glorify Him.

It was during that summer of 1991 that I began a project that the Lord would use to change every area of my life and change everything that I believed about living a Christian life. I wish that I could tell you that it was ignorance on my part that delayed my starting this project. Unfortunately, I had first heard of this principle almost fifteen years before I began applying it, and would hear it again on a regular basis at least once or twice a year. I suppose one could call it ignorance, if you define an ignorant person as one who <u>ignores</u> truth! That's about as good as my excuse gets. And, as we shall see, the Bible has this principle as one of its main themes. Therefore, that truth was before me for application during my entire life.

One would also think that, if I am a believer, I would see the number of times this principle is in Scripture and seen its importance. In fact, it is so important it should and <u>must</u> <u>be</u> considered as a <u>non-optional</u> principle to living a pure Christian life before the Lord. Now by non-optional I mean you don't have a choice. Terrible and foreign words are these to most believers, but especially to the American

Christian. "We live in the land of the free! And Christ has set us free! We always have a choice!" Now, of course, that is true; we do have a choice. But where we go wrong is in forgetting (or ignoring) that our choices <u>always</u> have consequences. The unvoiced and unthought assumption is that as a Christian, Christ must cover our every fault and problem, and that whatever we do has no consequences because we are "in Christ." <u>Absolutely</u> <u>nothing</u> could be further from the truth! James 4:17 tells us (as does the entire Sermon on the Mount) that "the one who knows the right thing to do and does not do it, to him it is sin." We may not like that or believe it, but to prove its accuracy, simply violate one of God's Laws and observe the consequences. Murder (hate) and see if your life will not be affected. Commit adultery (lust) and watch every area of your life being touched. Serve other gods (money, possessions, pleasure) and watch your spouse and children learn to love selfish pleasure over loving others (including you). Dishonor your parents (or your mate's parents) and observe the strife in your generation and your children's generation. Make provision for the flesh and note that that lust continues with its hold over you. The great book of Galatians, the book which was specifically written to warn us against our fleshly attempts to justify ourselves to God, is also the book that verifies to us that God's ways are non-optional: "Do not be deceived, God is not mocked; for whatever a man sows, this he will also reap. For the one who sows to his own flesh shall from the flesh reap corruption, but the one who sows to the spirit shall from the spirit reap eternal life." Please remember: the book of Galatians was not written to the lost; it was written to the believer. It is to me that he says, "Do not be deceived" because I am the one who, with my life, will violate God's Law by thinking I will not receive any discipline for doing so because I am "saved." It is I, the Christian, who falls for the deception that, because I am a Christian, I can do what I will without worry of consequences, that if I sow to the flesh I will still reap only the benefits of being a Christian. It is God's mercy and long-suffering that allows us to live and not be immediately destroyed. It is also our lack of belief in the principle of sowing and reaping that is the basis for our deception. ⏤ When our families fail, when our finances hopelessly collapse, when a child succumbs to immorality, when we watch the next generation involved in pleasure centered lives ruled only by destructive pursuits, know this: the seed was sown by us long ago. A farmer does not reap immediately. The crop takes time to develop. The seed sown long ago will <u>always</u> produce after its kind: a mature crop of the flesh or a mature crop of life. There are ways to uproot the evil sown, but understand: by the time we see the fruit of the crop we have sown, it is too late to fully stop its required growth. Notice also that God only gives us two choices: flesh and corruption or spirit and eternal life. If you are a Christian, eternal life has already begun. We are to be <u>only</u> sowing to the spirit; attempting to mix the spirit and the flesh is not a choice He has given us.

I recently attended a conference in which I had a conversation with a chaplain in the armed forces. He told me a story of a military exercise in which different branches of the service were working together. A group from one branch with an officer of another was acting as forward observers for planes dropping bombs. A mistake was made and a bomb was dropped close to where these men were standing. One of the men saw the bomb dropping and shouted, "In coming!" Those who were trained immediately threw themselves to the ground. The soldier from the other branch turned to see what the yelling was about. It was the last thing he did. God's principles appear to be a lot of trouble. And besides that, usually, everything is really okay. Why should we bother with a disciplined life? Why deny myself the things I want? God's principles appear optional—until the bomb drops. And know, just as the drill sergeant who trains soldiers to move immediately at the sound of their commander's voice knows—the bomb <u>will</u> drop! God's principles are non-optional. The soldier's opinion of training means nothing; the fact that day after day is calm and boring and without seen danger means nothing. The preservation of his life and those around him depend on his yielding to the training as non-optional. The soldier in day-to-day life sees no danger. But each new day may send him into a life and death struggle. Likewise, the Christian protected and blessed by God, comfortable with day to day life, Sunday to Sunday church, relying on the youth group and Sunday school to teach our children spiritual things, spending more time with gratification than with God, <u>cannot</u> afford to ignore the truths of God's Word—the bomb will drop!

Please do not think I am discounting God's grace and mercy. But we are deceived and mocking God if we discount His justice, righteousness, and holiness. Jesus did not negate these qualities of God with His sacrifice; He confirmed and established them. And if God is not holy and just and righteous or concerned with judgment then He is very cruel, for He killed His son for no reason.

God's ways become more apparently non-optional when we are desperate. A life preserver on a ship is not given any particular place of honor or attention until one is sinking in the water. It is the same with God and His ways. We are often not very interested until we become desperate. A desperate person will try just about anything. Unfortunately, most of us are not as much desperate as we are in despair. And a person in despair does nothing—because he believes nothing works. A person in despair is concerned with self-accomplishments in this world (i.e., his own reputation) and gaining peace through control of situations and people around him. And, as such, the things that are meaningful, lasting, and that require true death to self-exaltation and ambition are avoided. In Ecclesiastes 2:18-20 we see Solomon looking back over his life and being very honest for our sakes. "Thus I hated all the fruit of my labor for which I had labored under the sun, for I must leave it to the man who will come after me and who knows whether he will be a wise man or a fool? Yet he will have control over all the fruit of my labor for which I have labored by acting wisely under the sun. This too is vanity. Therefore I completely despaired of all the fruit of my labor for which I had labored under the sun." Notice his frenzied labor, the use of "I, me, my" 10 times, his emphasis on his control, and the despair of a man who "has it all." And the son to whom he left all—was the fool he feared. The most common mode of avoidance is the busy-ness mentioned earlier. It is much easier to be involved in activity than to be involved in accomplishment. The paradox is this: because he has come to the belief that nothing works, the person who is in despair, no matter how busy he may be, actually does nothing. Everything he does is nothing. And is designed to keep one step ahead of the facts—that he is failing in his faith and with family and that constant activity is the only anesthetic for the despair that awaits if he stops and faces reality. A person in despair is focused on self and self's abilities. A person that is desperate is grasping for something beyond self; is reaching for the lifeline; is asking, seeking, knocking. His eyes are off his own wishes and abilities and surrendered to another's wishes and abilities (poor in spirit); he accepts that past reliance on self and busyness for God was total failure (mourn); he realizes that his own strength has not and will not prevail and that another strength must save him (meekness); he begins to hunger and thirst for God's opinion of righteousness, rather than his own or that taught by a compromised clergy.

A desperate person is willing to seize the full and true gospel, the gospel taught by Jesus Christ. Today's church teaches a one-pronged gospel: "The kingdom of heaven is at hand." While that is true, it is not the complete gospel and leads to a man-centered, comfort-seeking church in which anything goes and everything is "just fine." But Christ did not present the gospel in this way. He and John the Baptist before Him presented the complete truth for desperate souls: "Repent, for the kingdom of heaven is at hand." Busy-ness is not repentance. More will be said regarding this later, but for now the point is that repentance is simply not taught or required anymore. The church doesn't teach it, and we as individuals avoid it. A person focused on "self" cannot repent. They are looking for someone to blame. And a comfort seeking church will not bring up repentance too often, as it may make people think they have done something wrong and therefore, "feel" uncomfortable. And that will never do! And so, the despair continues. Only those who are desperate repent and enter the kingdom. We in despair hear the kingdom of heaven is at hand and smile our contented smiles, believing we are, "rich, and have become wealthy, and have need of nothing, and yet do not know we are wretched and miserable and poor and blind and naked."

The portrait of despair as painted by my lack of peace and stability was a mixture of clashing colors. My outward appearance of gushy, emotionalism hungrily looking for the next "feel-good" experience hid an angry, cold heart with no true joy. My gaudy, religious frame took attention away from the drab colors of a temporal value system. My rigidity and judgment of others whitewashed my opinion that God's laws were too rigid and judgmental. An overemphasis on "grace" and "love" (as defined by myself for the current compromise) was all the excuse I needed to de-emphasized God's holiness, commands, and sovereignty. I talked of and exalted "faith", but oddly enough, lacked any true faith in God. I lacked wisdom, but was unteachable. I avoided personal, God-given responsibility, but was overbearing and demanding of others.

The whole of this chapter and the whole of my life is explained so clearly in the first chapter of the book of James. "But if any of you *lacks wisdom* (constant confusion), let him *ask of God* (no prayer life), who gives to all generously and *without reproach* (no understanding of the character of God), and it will be given to him but he must ask in *faith* (I had none) without any doubting (internal peace is compromised by compromise), for the one who doubts is like the surf of the sea, *driven and tossed* by the wind (every new wind of doctrine, non-doctrine, fad, teacher, error, or personal desire was my divided driving force), for that man *ought not to expect* that he will receive anything from the Lord, being a double-minded man, unstable in all his ways (a faith based on feelings and personal whim does not think).

This is certainly who I was before I began this non-optional project. Desperation led me to it. But even my desperation did not reveal to me the depth of my wretchedness, misery, poverty, blindness, and nakedness. But as I applied this principle, Jesus led me to joy beyond any imagination. But He first led me, as a Christian, to the understanding of repentance and the true picture of myself;

to see my complete poverty in every area. And how and why I had become so.

Chapter 2
The Double-minded Dilemma

This principle is not only non-optional; it is <u>the</u> principle on which true success as a Christian is based. Now, I know that some would react to such a statement, even without knowing the principle of which I speak. "Who is this man to judge whether I am a successful Christian?"...and, they would be right. But I did not say that this principle is the one on which true success as a Christian is based. God did. This leads us to a fact which must be dealt with before we go any further. I believe that the Bible is God's Word to mankind. I have had my fill of my opinion, mankind's opinion, higher education's opinion, higher criticism's opinion. I do not care about your theology. Please don't get too angry--I don't care about mine either. I do care about God's. And do not think by those words that I know His theology. While Scripture may say I have the mind of Christ, I also still have my own mind (which certainly muddles things considerably). But I do want to know His theology. And my belief is that His theology is contained in the Bible. And this work will be based, by His Grace, on His Word and not my opinion or another man's. I am not trying to be combative or arrogant in my stating this. But I think we all must look closely at our behaviors and thoughts, the behaviors and thoughts of others, at mankind's history and governments and realistically conclude—they have not worked. As it has been for all ages, God's Word is the only way to truth in life. Our opinion has never had the slightest effect on His truth.

As to my knowledge of this principle's effect on Christian success I cannot say that I knew or believed it. Not that I had not heard it many times before. But in my hearing was also ignoring. When I began to pursue the principle as a project I had no idea what the fruit of such a project would be. I did know that I was desperate. And it was that desperation which began to drive me. For, you see, some one in despair simply sits, believing that all is hopeless, and will not move, no matter what the council or help offered. They drain the energies of many trying to help them become whole. But it is the desperate one who can be reached. A desperate person will grasp at the smallest hope and cling for dear life. In that desperation I reached for this last straw. To prove to myself whether Christianity was a fraud and that I had been duped for many years, or to find the reality I believed must be there. I found very quickly that Christianity was not the fraud—I was. Because, as I began to apply this truth of God, He was "as good as His Word", responding to the promise He had made that I alone had failed to appropriate.

The first indication that something had changed was in the one area I never would have predicted. The reason I would not have predicted a change in this area is that I had rarely seen such changes in my life or in the lives of others. That was the area of victory over sin.

To some of us that may be a new concept. The era of the "seeker friendly church" that relegates the cross and repentance to the back rooms in the church building and preaches a gospel of "Jesus died to make you happy!" knows little of freedom from sin. "Christian liberty" has become a license to sin. The book of Phillipians written today would read, "I can do all things through Christ that pleaseth me." It is little wonder that we cannot understand the joy expressed by earlier writers and hymnists, when they speak of freedom from sin as some wondrous miracle and a freedom from an unspeakable bondage. The concept taught in today's congregations, that happiness is my freedom to do anything I wish, is a heresy which would never have been tolerated and is as far from their Biblically based lives as peace and simplicity are from ours. And, unexpectedly, this miracle for which millions have sought and many despaired, had come upon me.

And it was a miracle! I had experienced little freedom over sin in my life. I am not speaking here just of the sins which may trip one unexpectedly. I'm talking about the one that always wins. You know the one. The secret one; the uncontrollable one; the one you actually see coming; the big hole in the road into which you always crash. My strength had never effected victory. But now, unexpectedly, instead of the predictable failure, the temptation would be suddenly past me with no more effect on me as if it had been a passing, unremembered breeze. This began to be a common occurance and as I was completely baffled--almost frustrated by what I could not understand--I eventually asked God what had happened to me. His short quiet reply, which will be discussed later, left me shocked at how little attention I, as a Christian, had really given to His Word.

I very clearly remember the day the Lord allowed me to see why this project had begun to produce the things which I believed Christianity to be. I was waiting at a church building for one of those many meetings I mentioned earlier. I was passing time thinking about some Scripture and a very familiar section came to mind. It was so familiar that I was about to put it out of my mind when I heard the Lord's voice in me saying "I thought you were going to look at *all* My Word." As I began to look at this passage, a deeper truth began to emerge that I had not seen before. The reason for my failure to live the Christian life unfolded before me as one of the major themes of the Bible. And it was here that I truly saw that "<u>every</u> word of God is tested," for what appeared to be the most insignificant words in this verse became the key to understanding. The passage is Matthew 6: 22-24:

22. The light of the body is the eye; if therefore thine eye be single, thy whole

body shall be full of light.

23. But if thine eye be evil, thy whole body shall be full of darkness. If, therefore the light that is in thee be darkness, how great is that darkness.

24. No man can serve two masters; for either he will hate the one, and love the other; or else he will hold to the one and despise the other. You cannot serve God and mammon."

At first glance these verses may appear unrelated, but God's Word is full of hidden treasure, and a closer look shows how closely connected they really are.

When Jesus tells us, "The light of the body is the eye," He is telling us that we view life--and act accordingly--through our belief system. We make judgments about situations and people with such rapidity that they really must be considered a reflex. Our reactions are immediate, with little or no thought. Because what we believe in our heart or our inner man is what motivates us to act. The way we react and behave and speak is not usually dictated by thought processes at that moment. The thought processes and patterns developed long before the event, and those thoughts become our belief system, which then dictates our behavior and speech. We drive over bridges. We do not stop at each bridge, test it with scientific instruments, and then decide to drive on it. We drive over bridges without even slowing down because we have come to believe that bridges will hold us up.

It is no different with our day to day behaviors and personalities. I behave the way I behave because I have believed that particular behaviors will help me, protect me, feed me, or make others like me; and I came to these conclusions long before I needed help, needed protection, was hungry, or met someone I wished to impress. And so, as with the bridge, I do not stop in day-to-day activity to slowly test and formulate my next action. I simply behave-- dictated, controlled, and willed by a belief system whose existence is no more noticed by me than a puppet does its puppeteer. And even when I do stop to formulate certain actions, that formulation will be controlled by what I already believe to be true.

We often believe that which makes us comfortable, without knowing that the very reason we believe it is that it make us comfortable. My conscience will make me feel uncomfortable when I violate God's Law. To stop this uncomfortable feeling I must, either agree with God's Law and conform to it or, in some way, overrule my conscience. Retrain it. Make it believe "what works for me." Become a law to myself and reject God's Moral Law as too strict. And it is in this way we see that past moral failures dictate current beliefs. My philosophy is not that which dictates my morality, but rather it is my morality which dictates my philosophy. Which again brings us to our belief system. My morality or lack of it dictates the makeup of my belief system. And that belief system controls my actions.

But before we go further this belief system must be more clearly defined. And the definition of my belief system is not so much defined as *what* it is, but rather, *where* it is. Because it is what I believe with my mind that I hope, think, and say I believe--but it is that which I believe in my heart that my actions will speak louder than words. For it is a spiritual and psychological law--I will mentally and verbally assent to what I want to believe, but I will always act out what I truly believe. There is belief with the mind; and there is belief with the heart. Please do not think I am about to define this "heart." It probably will never be defined or even recognized "scientifically," and mine is certainly not the mind to do so theologically. Some may call it the spirit, others the center of our soul. Whatever it may be, for one reason only, we must accept its existence and its function in containing the deepest of our beliefs--the Bible tells us so. For while Scripture speaks rarely of the physical heart, it uses the word "heart" hundreds of times to refer to the seat of belief. And a quick study of the word as used in the Bible will show that the beliefs and thoughts of the heart subjugate and overpower those of the mind and that actions and intent come from the heart.

So, the light of the body is the eye; life is viewed and lived through our belief system. But Jesus makes a distinction between two kinds of belief systems. "If thine eye be single...".The Greek word *hapious* gives the meaning of "simplicity, singleness, or the absence of folds."[1] It is pure, clear, unwavering. It is belief produced by a singleness of heart toward God, which fills the life with the light of truth. And then He gives the contrast. "But if thine eye be evil, thy whole body will be full of darkness." If my view of life, my belief system, is in rebellion to God's Law, twisted and unfocused on the singleness of life in the Creator God, then my entire life will always be tainted with that evil. I will never be free from selfishness, greed, lust, pride, and the uncontrollable drives which come with them. Titus 1:15

---

[1]The Complete Word Study Dictionary, Zodhiates, p.1808

gives us the picture, "Unto the pure all things are pure; but unto them that are defiled and unbelieving is nothing pure; but even their mind and conscience is defiled." But, returning to our Lord's words, it is actually much worse. He then tells us that if our belief system--the light that is in us--is darkness, that the end result of that darkness is that we will view lies as truth, truth as lies--and never know we are doing so. My heart, so full of lies, will readily believe lies. And healing, saving truth will be rejected as that which would cause me harm. To me, this is one of the most frightening pictures and fates I can possibly imagine. A person in this position is the most needy person in this world. And yet, if given the very truth he needs for life, it actually repulses him. And the darkness in which he believes is so great, it is never seen by them as darkness. And this person follows that darkness confidently--into eternity.

At first glance, it would appear that Jesus now changes subjects. But viewed more closely He actually has described the two belief systems in life and now begins to describe our attempts to serve those two systems simultaneously. "No one can serve two masters." First we must understand there are no exceptions: "No one." While I may believe I am the exception, that belief is opposite of God's truth and is thereby a lie. But the true emphasis of this sentence is on service. One who tries to serve two masters may be very busy, but their service will be ineffective, nothing more than clouds without rain. Why this must be is very simple to ascertain. A master is an absolute authority. And equal authorities never have the same goals. History, governments, business, industry, families, and nature all bear witness to this fact. Only one master is allowed, one head. Never are there never two kings, two presidents, two chief executive officers. Even in the curiosities of nature, such as a two-headed snake, one head is always subservient to the other. True and profitable service to one master will be compromised with attempted loyalty to another. And when these loyalties are in conflict, they are lies, and compromise must result, thereby bringing about ineffectual service. This verse specifically tells me why my frenzy is not fruitful. If I am attempting to give my "whole life" to God, but also spend part of that "whole life" in pursuit of mammon, I cannot and will not be wholly serving God, and I will not be a success in my Christian life. With my mouth I say I belong to God. With my life I testify that I belong to me.

To add deeper understanding let us look at the word *mammon*. According to Vines Expository Dictionary of New Testament Words, *mammon* is an "Aramaic word for riches, akin to a Hebrew word signifying to be firm, steadfast, hence, that which is to be trusted." In short, it signifies a faith in the ways and things of the world and, is therefore, the opposite of faith in the ways and things of God. Jesus is saying "One must have faith in the world or in God. Your faith will dictate your actions, and therefore, the value of your service. Compromised service is service of no value to God---or even the world."

The final phrase in this verse is a Law and Commandment, spoken into being by the Son of God. It is not open for discussion or opinion. It is the final word on compromise with anything of this world. "Ye cannot serve God and mammon." And please, please note—He only gives two choices. One of the greatest follies of mankind is using our imagination combined with our arrogance to create a "third choice" which exists, not in reality, but only in personal fantasy. Time after time after time God gives only two choices—we chose a third. God offers light or darkness—we chose gray. God offers life or death—we chose both.   God offers hot or cold—we chose lukewarm. God offers good or evil—we chose compromise. Gray, lukewarm, compromise is judged by God to be what they truly are—continued sin, violation of covenant, walking in darkness.

But it is the central part of this verse which conceals an insight that is one of the major themes of the Bible. Jesus tells us, "for either he will hate the one, and love the other; or else he will hold to the one, and despise the other." Here I must admit to a very superficial reading of the Bible. For I had often read these verses, often heard these verses. But I had not listened. How often I have thought the Bible boring or not understandable! But the problem was me, not God's Word. The things of God are given to those who ask, seek, and knock, not those who merely hear.

When reading these verses my thoughts had always been that Jesus was using a parallelism—a repeating of the same thought using different words to make a point more understandable. But this was from my typical Western mind set of attempting to understand with my mind rather than from God's spirit. As I began to meditate on His statement I began to see that often the smallest, most insignificant appearing words hold the key to understanding the truth.

Jesus says "for <u>either</u>." He is talking about choices. He gives only two and excludes all others. "For either he will" is a predictive matter of fact; it will happen as Jesus says. I cannot change that. He then gives us the two choices.   Note His use of conjunctions to divide the two choices. "For either he will

    1. hate one **and** love the other

or

    2. hold to one **and** despise the other".

The word *or* is an exclusive conjunction indicating separate possession or action (e.g. 'I have an apple or an orange.' I have one <u>or</u> the other, not both). This word separates and defines the two choices we are given. But within the two choices is the word *and*, which is an inclusive conjunction indicating simultaneous possession or action (e.g. 'I have an apple <u>and</u> an orange.' I possess both simultaneously.).

Choice number one is easy to understand. Love vs. hate. Unfortunately, as we shall see, it is not such an easy choice to make. The Greek word for love used here is *agape*, which is the purist, highest form of love, focused only on the good of the one loved, excluding all others. The Greek word for hate is *miseo*, which simply defined is the opposite of *agape*. While *agape* is complete subjection to the good of the one loved, *miseo* is complete rejection of the one hated. Simply stated, Jesus is telling us that pure love is so powerful, so focused, that others do not exist. There is no competition. Because no other love exists in the mind and heart of the lover. Obviously, this is the option God desires. From the opening of Scripture to its end, it is clear He desires us to love Him with all our heart, soul, and might. But, oddly enough, if we will not love Him completely, He would rather we hate Him completely. He tells us this in Revelation 3:15 when He states that He would rather we be cold toward Him than lukewarm.

Which brings us to the second and only other choice we have: holding to one and despising the other. Again, Jesus is not simply describing or restating what he has previously said. He is giving the choice I <u>will</u> make by <u>not</u> choosing the first. For by not choosing, I choose. To be neither hot nor cold, I have by my stagnation chosen stagnancy.

While "holding to one" is viewed as love by our acceptance starved-society, it is in fact the mortal enemy of love---pure selfishness. My holding or clinging to someone is never the selflessness of *agape* love. The object of holding or clinging to someone is seeking my own satisfaction, my own lust, attempting to provoke a response for "me."

The words sound so good (and, therefore, "true") because they appeal to my own selfishness. Phrases such as, "I want you," "I need you," "Let me hold you," all sound loving. But a relationship which is defined by holding or clinging to a person is defined by the use of that person for selfish satisfaction. The focus is me—and no one else. Its focus is love—but love directed to me. Its meaning, given in the phrase "I love me, I want you." It is attachment, certainly, mixed with the appearance of affection. But attachment soon gives way to demand, expectation, and exploitation. Idolatry always does. A god or goddess created in my own image must eventually comply to my possessive will. So, while "holding to one" appears to be a positive disposition, its very nature is to despise the object of its false affection.

It is this mixture of illusory affection and despisement that is the problem. If I despise someone, I do not reject them. In fact, far from rejecting, they have become my emotional focus, albeit a negative emotional focus. As such, they occupy space in my heart and mind, and whether consciously or unconsciously is "on my mind." A person I despise may be used by me, looked down on by me, talked about, and laughed at, even enslaved—but not rejected. The connection remains. And in appearance, the despising is imperceptible from the holding. For the ultimate center around which these twin planets orbit is always self-service. And if I am serving self, I am not serving God or mammon. I have the appearance of service to both, with actual service to none. And the appearance of service is religion, not worship; not substance, but symbols; not commitment, but compromise.

Which has been the problem from man's beginning. Service to self calls for compromise. The very word *compromise* tells the tale of mankind---*com* and *promise*. The prefix *com* means together or jointly, and is combined with *promise*. Not promised to one, but promised to two. Not single-minded service to one God, but rather double-minded service to self. The use of God for the blessings He gives; the use of the world for the pleasures it brings. The despising of God by disobeying his commands; the despising of the world by obeying its ways, and thereby, bearing false witness of the requirements of a holy God.

So we see that the Lord has gives two choices in life: single-minded service or double-minded self service. One choice of such focused love that it excludes all others for self loss. The other with such focused selfishness, that it includes all only for self gain.

Chapter 3
The Single-minded Solution

It is obvious from all of Scripture that single-minded is what I should be, but double-minded is what I am. The very first temptation has this concept at its core. The tree, of which we all ate through Adam, was not the tree of knowing the difference *between* good and evil—it was the tree *of the knowledge* of good and evil, the tree of knowing good and evil simultaneously, the tree of double-mindedness. The universe decayed that day. Instability and death were chosen as lords, gods, and kings over mankind. It is interesting that the single-fruited tree of life was disregarded for the double-fruited tree of death. The history of mankind has become a documentation of constant confusion and compromise. Logic and love left hand in hand when Paradise became lost.

My true desire, of course, is that being of double-mind is not as bad as it has been presented; perhaps it is not as pervasive and as invasive as portrayed. But, the first chapter of James tells us that the double-minded man is unstable in *all* his ways. And the fourth chapter of the same book states that my impure heart comes from a double-mind: "purify your hearts, ye double minded." My arguments against myself are of no avail. The back and forth "Yes, I will"-"No, I won't" battles are fruitless incursions into what is truly "no-man's land." Jesus stated that the house divided against itself must fall. I am that house.

One of the saddest statements in all of Scripture comes from Deuteronomy 30:19, which says "I have set before you life and death, blessing and cursing: therefore choose life." How silly does God think we are? With life vs.

death and blessing vs. cursing before me as choices, of course I choose life and blessing!! The sad truth is just the opposite. — God knows His creatures well. We have consistently chosen death over life and cursing over blessing. Those who do not believe that statement globally need merely to read a newspaper or read a little history. Those who do not believe it personally need only to reflect (honestly) on the broken relationships, self inflicted struggles and losses, and the self-centered actions and words that have emanated from their own life. Those, who after personal reflection still do not believe so, need not trouble themselves to read further.

For it must be on a personal basis that I face double-mindedness; as it must also be on a personal basis that I seek the solution. "Blame" of others is merely another symptom substantiating the diagnosis. As already stated, God's solution for double-mindedness is single-mindedness, which is only rhetoric if unaccompanied by process. That procedure, God's answer to the dilemma of double-mindedness, is much of the good news of the gospel. But to appreciate the good news, we must first hear and appreciate the bad news. The gospel is never "the kingdom of heaven is at hand," rather it is "repent (first), the kingdom is at hand." The bad news of which I must repent is a life of double-mindedness; the false belief that the kingdom of heaven can exist in my life without repentance of my own compromise.

Unfortunately, I have an inaccurate picture of repentance in my mind. The word "repent" has not changed, but our understanding of it has. In the minds of many Christians the word "repent" has come to mean some type of emotional response to guilt or walking the church aisle after powerful oratory while the choir sings "just one more verse" of an invitational hymn. These actions may be or may not be a part of repenting, but an emotionally lead commitment is as unstable and as short-lived as the moment of emotion that produced it. In the Hebrew there are two words translated as "repent," both having the same essential meaning—to turn back, to turn around, to *change the mind*. The Greek word is even more direct with the meaning "to *change the mind*; relent."[2]

Certainly, emotions and sorrow may be a result of the changing of the mind, but to repent is not emotional—it is volitional. One of the oddest statements of which mankind is guilty is that of refusing to forgive, love, change, repent, or obey God's Law because "I don't feel it," believing that it would be hypocritical for me to do so if it is "not in my heart." What a gross misunderstanding of truth and grace! God commands me to do these things—not feel them! He will provide the strength that surpasses my understanding or passions. His Grace is sufficient—my emotions will never be so.

Therefore, I am commanded to "change my mind." Those words are among those that roll off the tongue, but never seem to stick in the brain. The changing of my mind usually involves only my comfort—not my belief system. And, I have often tried to change my mind about my sin and transgressions against God and others. Or at least, have attempted to change my behaviors. And as I attempt to change my behaviors, I find, as already stated, that my behaviors line up with my belief system. And my belief system lines up with my wishes and selfishnesses. Methods tried are tired and tiresome, and usually involve the oddity of my will over my will. It sounds as silly as it is. Declaring myself to be single-minded is akin to declaring myself to be a

---

[2] Strong's numbers Hebrew 7725, 5162 and Greek 3340. <u>AMG Complete Word Study Bible and Reference CD</u>; AMG Publishers

neurosurgeon. It is completely delusional. "Yes, I decided two weeks ago that I am a neurosurgeon and I have opened my office." That sentence will have the same impact on reality as my belief that I can "think" myself to single-mindedness.

Well, perhaps, I can resist my double-mindedness and not think on the sin that so easily overwhelms me. But that only makes it worse. For my "resisting" produces a certain mental focus—on the wrong thing. For to "resist" sin, I must focus on not thinking about what I do not want to think about, and thereby, think even more so on the problem!!! To illustrate, I want you to resist thinking about a white elephant. Probably, few reading this have even seen a white elephant. Yet, as soon as the suggestion is made to not think about a white elephant, the imagination immediately conjures a picture of the forbidden object. Paul stated in Romans "but sin, taking occasion by the commandment, wrought in me all manner of concupiscence (lust)." And such it is with sin. And such it always is with my attempts at resisting "the me" I have become.

Some, at this point, may be thinking I have left out the obvious answer of prayer. But true prayer must be in agreement with God. And I, with my double-mind, attempt to agree with God, while simultaneously disagree with God! My instability and lack of faith preclude any consistent answers to prayer.

And it is here that I give up. And this, of course, is what God had intended all along. His grace—not my will or wish—is acting upon my double-mind. But that acting is the desire and power to do His will. It is, and always will be, His power. But, that desire and power does produce action in and from me. That action is the non-optional project of which I spoke earlier. That action is abiding in the Written

Word, which, it is promised, brings relationship with the Creator. That action is placing God's Word in my mind through memorization and placing it in my heart through meditation. It is easy enough to remember—memorize and meditate—M and M's. "Man does not live by bread alone, but by God's" M and M's. —*every word.*

The concepts of memorizing and meditation on Scripture have been deemed passé by most of us now. Our concept of God's love has me at the center and often with no attesting action of love toward God or of a saved, changed life. Salvation is for Me. Heaven is for Me. God's blessings are for Me. God is for Me. I am for Me. Memorization of Scripture would require effort *from* Me. Empowered by Him, yes, but still effort—taking from My time, from My schedule, from My comfort. And these beliefs are My theology—Meology. Meditation is worse, as it requires Me to sit still. To listen to another voice—one that is not Me. Meditation does not appeal to my ego. It is not flashy. It may be dull! I might get bored!!

Have you noticed we have come full circle? The true choice is between God and Me. I want the third, but non-existent choice of pleasing both God and Me. Behind virtually every action, statement, and attitude is an unspoken, unconscious question: "Will this make me happy?" The two do not and cannot successfully mix. In Romans 7 Paul says "For I joyfully concur with the law of God in the inner man, but I see a different law in the members of my body, waging war against the law of my mind and making me a prisoner of the law of sin which is in my members." Two standards of measure exist; two laws; two natures: God's pleasure or man's pleasure. Revelation 4:11 states: "Thou art worthy, O Lord, to receive glory and honor and power: for thou hast created all things, and for *thy pleasure* (or will) they are and were created." So, I continue to be confronted with His grace, for His pleasure, producing action in me, defined by Him. And part of that definition, as will be shown, is abiding in His Word through meditation.

Romans 11:36 to 12:2 states it like this: "For from Him and through Him and to Him are all things. To Him be the glory forever. Amen. Therefore I urge you, brethren, by the mercies of God, to present your bodies a living and holy sacrifice, acceptable to God, which is your spiritual service of worship. And do not be conformed to this world, but be transformed by the renewing of your mind, so that you may prove what the will of God is, that which is good and acceptable and perfect" First, we are reminded of the reason for all things—Him. And here we are told that as Believers our service to God, just that which is reasonable—not overly demanding—is that I be holy and a living sacrifice with my body. The word holy means, in its simplest state "separate," which is the next thought of this passage: "do not be conformed to this world." Again, we are given two choices—holiness (separation from the world) versus conformity to this world. We are not given the double-minded choice of both. But with this choice we are also given the solution: "but be transformed by the renewing of your mind." The answer to conformity with the world is transformity of the mind, by its renewal—with its filling with the perfect will of God—His Word.

↗ But why memorize? Why meditate? Won't reading God's Word do? Certainly, we must read God's Word. We are told in Scripture to do so. And it brings great joy, comfort, and direction. But will it truly renew my mind? There is a very serious problem with just reading: I forget what I read. No matter how much time I spend devoting to devotionals, my behavior is rarely affected by it. Because I forget!!! Because, while I agree with my mind, I find that I do not agree in my heart. And day-to-day life happens upon me and to me, and I do not do as I wish. Most of my behavior is reflexive, not reflective. I do not do as I purpose to do. And I am not alone. Romans 7:19 states, "For the good that I want, I do not do, but I practice the very evil that I do not want." James 1 states the same thing, expanding a bit on the same theme: "But prove yourselves doers of the word, and not merely hearers who delude themselves. For if anyone is a hearer of the word and not a doer, he is like a man who looks at his natural face in a mirror; for once he has looked at himself and gone away, he has immediately forgotten what kind of person he was, but one who looks intently at the perfect law, the law of liberty, and abides by it, not having become a forgetful hearer but an effectual doer, this man will be blessed in what he does." Hearing the Word and not doing the Word is deception of self. The picture is exact. I read, I observe my need to change, I leave my devotion time, I forget my devotion time—I remain the same, unchanged.

In Ephesians 4 we see Paul stating again the theme of renewal of the mind as an answer to problems of the heart: "So this I say, and affirm together with the Lord, that you walk no longer just as the Gentiles also walk, in the futility of their mind being darkened in their understanding, excluded from the life of God because of the ignorance that is in them, because of the hardness of their heart...and that you be renewed in the spirit of your mind, and put on the new self, which in the likeness of God has been created in righteousness and holiness of the truth" Just as our spirit must be born from above, the spirit of our mind must be renewed. It is the futility of the mind that alienates me from the life of God. We are almost daily bombarded with an idea that sounds so good, that it must be true: quality of life. While quality of life is a nice concept, it is not a Biblical concept. Suffering, the Cross, death to self, and being the servant of all do not allow for the seeking of quality of life. For it is not quality of life that God seeks for us—it is a life of quality. And that is found in the new man in righteousness and true holiness by the renewal of the spirit of my mind through the Word of God.

My mind, with help from the mind of the father of lies, can readily find many excuses to rationalize what has been said thus far. And, if I allow myself, and my unrecognized confederate to keep the resistance on the level of superficial preference, the true infection, the intimacy that is my design and desire, will continue to be my dread.

Chapter 4
Intimidating Intimacy

Despite designed arguments and designed experiments, which are designed to help me see design as accident, God's Word continues to say, "created", as does the evidence around me, scientific or otherwise. If I am an evolutionary accident, I am purposeless, as are those around me. And it is fitting that I use those other purposeless accidents for my own purposes—my egotistical or lustful gratifications. Unfortunately, if I am also purposeless, it is also fitting that they use me in a similar fashion. Perhaps this is the best objective evidence for evolution—purposeless mankind is bestial at best.

But there are also those elite purposes; those purposes that appear to be of a "higher calling", that in like manner display the brute that is "I". For egotistical gratification is easily expressed in evangelism, through judgment of those outside my particular brand of elitism (or electism). From denominational damnations to exclusionary eschatologies—all are part of the armor I take up. Is the churchgoer's outcry against those deemed unfit due to petty differences any different than the evolutionist's outcry of "survival of the fittest?" Most of the divisions between Believers are beliefs over which they have no control—they are the jurisdiction of God, not mankind. Do I have any power or say so over election, condemnation, judgment, the end times, free will, or God's means of salvation? Is my true armor the breastplate of self-righteousness? And are the weapons of my warfare actually used for pulling down people—those for whom Messiah died—saved or unsaved, elected or free willed, Jew or Gentile, Muslim or Mennonite? Are my feet actually shod with preparation to tread on others and the helmet of salvation donned to protect my closed, narrow mind from a God's heart and love that is so large the entire universe cannot contain it? The shield of religion is easier to wield and more convenient than that of faith—and very able to quench any darts of truth, love, and acceptance, which the Holy Spirit might aim from the direction of the commandment that I am to "love one another." It is the Christian Religion that has hated and killed Jew and Muslim, Protestant and Catholic in the name of Christ. If my God requires me to protect and save him, He is too weak to protect and save me.

It is the armor of religion that protects me so well from the God who has stalked me through eternity. That destruction is not the trappings of organized religion with its pride, which so neatly fits me. That destruction is the final destruction of me, fully sickened of self and swallowed up by the Life of God. It is the thing for which I have been created, and is my purpose. It is my greatest fear—and the deeply hidden yearning behind every twisted passion of my soul.

When I began to memorize and meditate upon God's Word, I had no idea that there was anything about God except religion. Certainly, I had heard, from time to time, other ideas, but I could not and would not understand what was being said. I was in control with my religion. Religion is man's attempts to control God. And I was about to lose control—and gain life.

Meditation requires certain aloneness. Whether in a crowd or abandoned by all, I must be alone—with God. My beginnings of meditation were clumsy at best. I knew little of my new business, except desperation. But God's Spirit called me, and enabled me to be alone—with God.

And He was there.

That was quite a shock. My Creator went from a theoretical entity to a very real Presence. And there was no particular reason, which I could tell, that it should be so. To a mind trained to bow at the sound of the mantras of naturalism and organized religion, the realness of The Presence refused to correspond to the evidence. For Creator has never bowed to the evidentiary demands of creature, offering even to a skeptical and fearful Moses being sent to an enslaved and despondent Israel only the fact of Existence—I AM.

The shock was the Realness—the Unexpected. For there was no excuse for The Presence—no "worship" cheerleaders as spirit guides, no robed melodramas from the trained Diviners Elite, no current best-selling book to drive my life, no expectations, no instability, no emotions—just the unshakeable Realness; reaching Light into the darkness that was me. There are those who will immediately react with the accusation of "Experiential religion"!!! And certainly there is "experience" in this testimony of my life. To be wary of testimony and experience is Biblical and wise; to discount them is un-Biblical and dead. Extra-Biblical experience should not be confused or combined with un-Biblical experience. Extra-Biblical experience can certainly be untrue, but it is not necessarily untrue. Do we not see in the book of The Revelation of Jesus Christ that "they overcame him by the blood of the Lamb and the word of their testimony"? Millions come to true faith in Christ as they "experience" His saving power of the salvation of their soul or the re-birth of their dead life. Did Paul, Peter, John, Isaiah, Abraham, David, the Emmaus road disciples, Mary and Joseph, and the centurion at the cross not experience Christ? From creation to the cries of the Spirit and the bride of "Come", the Bible gives testimony to the experiencing of

Christ. Of course, the very use of the term "experiential religion" is quite telling. Religion does not love God—religion loves itself. It is far more the fear of relationship than the fear of God that generates the judgment of "experiential religion". Jesus stated that no man having drunk old wine desires new for he says the old is better. Religious wine is certainly high in intoxicating content and satiates the ego. But it is the trading of that which truly satisfies for that which merely intoxicates and blurs the judgment. My old religion is "better" than the real Relationship, for its demands of worship are the hymns sung in agreement from the heart; praises for my performance whitewashed with the name of Christ.

Man's greatest fear is actually the standard of measure by which he will be judged—Christ knowing him on a personal level (Matthew 7:23). For true relationship does not demand my ego, it demands no ego; it does not demand my strength, it demands no strength. It is here that I see the fear of the Lord; for it is in a true love relationship that I know I will be displaced and the life I live to self and for self will die. My unseen, but most real Fear is of love, and God is love. Love is the Timeless Self inserting itself into My Time. And as such, the requirement from me is not time, but my Self; which, as stated earlier, is turning away from all my busy-ness and turning to face the fear of quietness. And it was here that I met, deep in my soul, my fear, my longing and My God.

But how does one "meet" God? I am afraid the answer lies in the miraculous and mystical. Before the more "conservative" reader finds another excuse to run from such heresy I ask that you consider a few facts. Paul states in the third chapter of Galatians, "This is the only thing I want to find out from you: did you receive the Spirit by the works of the Law, or by hearing with faith?" and "does He who provides you with the Spirit and works miracles among you, do it by the works of the Law, or by hearing with faith?" Jesus states in John 3, "That which is born of the flesh is flesh, and that which is born of the Spirit is spirit. Do not be amazed that I said to you, 'You must be born again.' The wind blows where it wishes and you hear the sound of it, but do not know where it comes from and where it is going; so is everyone who is born of the Spirit.."

Was the incarnation miraculous? Do I know how an eternal spirit impregnated a mortal woman? Is there something of the mysterious in Messiah's birth? If you are "born again", how did you become so?" Was it by your religion? Did you work it so? Was it in your power? Did you give birth to yourself? I think not. It was a miracle—a mysterious miracle. Or have you noticed how often the word "mystery" is used to describe the gospel? We know far too little and are far too little to relegate the mechanism of the new birth to our level of understanding. True miracles are outside of our ability to understand—they just are. True faith in God is always based on the miraculous and the mysterious. It is otherwise dead and useless religion.

Is there any description of spiritual fellowship with God that physical, human words can encompass? How can one speak of the inward peace mixed with delight and anticipation? Finding peace in religion is not possible, as religion has as its constant demand the next task I must perform to be approved of by God or to pay Him back for what he has done; relationship in God is allowing Him to be, leaving me simply sitting at His feet, listening to Him, for Him, in Him, by Him. I not only had peace, but, yes, an emotional filling that satisfied the dark, lonely, vacuous cry that had always been my soul. The Biblical writers seem intense about such things as we see time after time words such as "with Christ", "in His presence", "abide in Me"—statements pertaining to the here and now; addressed to buried emotions and answering the most common bond of our ancestral aloneness. He answers all with Himself.

And miraculously and mysteriously, God met me. The word "fellowship" had been simply a word one read or said. That was no longer to be so in my life, for I was now meeting with God in a way I had not believed possible. My "place" of meditation at that time was a small room where I could close the door and sit quietly before the Lord. That was a true blessing; a mighty convenience. Many of the greatest saints have learned meditation on urine-muddied floors of crowded prison cells, the frozen night walls of labor camps, or as they lay dying, tortured by man and sun, purified into light by the Son.

I would retire to my "sanctuary" and find that God's presence made my inner self the sanctuary. As I meditated on His Word, I began to hear the voice of God in that inner sanctuary. And He began to hear me. He began to answer my questions. He began to show me the hidden me; the true intent of my self that was set only on self. My sanctimonious self-centeredness had stifled the building of a true sanctuary. Jesus stepped into His rightful temple; it was not violent, but it was firm. He began cleansing the temple. Repentance became a way of life as the Lord began to show me where I had substituted my own way for His, and separated myself from him, others, and even myself. Romans 7:7 states, "...I had not known sin but by the Law..." and I John 3:4 states, "...sin is the transgression of the law." It is God's law that defines sin. It is His law that exposes sin. This is why men react to God's law. Even those in the "church" have declared us "free from the Law," as if Christ's death had cancelled the Law rather than the debt. My freedom from the Law is Christ's life of victoriously living the Law; and that life now lives in me. Jesus did not live the law to have His life within me violate the law. He lived the law in His body on earth. The gospel is that He still has the power to live that Law in His body on earth; that body is the true church.

Allowing God to look at me from the standpoint of His righteousness was, of course, very uncomfortable. But it must be realized: He was always looking upon me from the standpoint of His righteousness!! The difference now was that I was looking with Him. The discomfort was not God knowing something about me; it was that I now knew what He knew. We love the imagery of Jesus as light, lighting my path in the darkness. But it is not the path that is dark—it is me; the eyes of my understanding have been darkened. Without The Light I cannot see light. And with more light, I see more light. To hear the voice of God's Holy Spirit telling me where I had and was missing the mark became as natural as hearing the voice of my mother. That voice gently led me to see a grief unobserved. And to repentance before God, and before many of His creatures I had used as my own subjects for my pleasures or rages. And His empowerment to me to respond in repentance to His voice led me to freedom. He unlocked and lit the cell of my solitary confinement, which Fear had promised would be a fountain of friendship and liberty. Old habits, selfish attitudes, destructive speech, perverse thoughts; those giants I had never slain, quietly left through the pinprick from which they had come. I was no longer blind!! I could see who I really was and the way others saw me!! That is fearful—unless one is being held by the hand of Love. With this "new found" friend, I had the confidence to face myself without fear, and to admit my often wrongs.

My first order of business was clearing my conscience with my God. It was His law I had violated. It was relationship with Him I had disdained. But He quickly led me to His creatures; God most often measures my violation of His law by my violation of His creatures. And in doing so it was relationship with them I had also disdained. God's voice time after time led me to memories of how I had hurt, used, and offended others. My heart broke at the viewing of my self-centeredness and arrogance. But I knew the tears of my anguish did not equal those of the one's I had violated. It became a way of life to admit wrong; to go to those who I had hurt and humble myself, admitting my wrong, and asking, begging their forgiveness. And there were many. I did not spend my time in introspection—it is the Holy Spirit who is to search me—"Search me O God."

As I became less and less encumbered by sin, my fellowship with God grew deeper and closer. Stepping quickly into His presence became the norm for my life. One day, as I sat in a small room with doors and windows closed and lights off, His presence was more real than I had ever imagined it could be. By this time I had learned that one of the things that sets a disciple apart to His Master was the asking of questions—and I sensed that He was inviting me to do just that. All I could say was "What is it, Lord?" His answer came, not audibly but deep in my understanding, as if a voice had bypassed my ears and entered my mind. He said, "Every Sunday you go to church and hug your brothers. There is one you have not hugged." My quick assumption, knowing my heart and failings, was that I was acting superior to someone and not treating them with honor. I asked "Who, Lord?" He answered, "Me." This did not fit my theology.

A flood of thoughts rushed through my mind as I tried to assimilate His answer. "It is not the Lord", "it is my imagination", "Why am I not afraid?" It was an invitation for which, my soul had forever unconsciously longed—it is perfect love that casts out fear. But, I will admit I was glad the doors were closed, the lights were out, and I was very much alone.

In faith, I opened my arms—and closed them—around a physical body—as arms also wrapped themselves around me. It only lasted a moment. I fell forward weeping—stunned over what had just happened. Amazed, confused, barely able to think or register any emotion except that of being completely overwhelmed by the Unthinkable and the Unexpected. Please understand: this happened only this one time and as of this writing has not happened again. It was not at an emotionally charged meeting, nor could I have even remotely imagined such a thing happening. Emotion and imagination are ruled out as "causes." Of course, while it is good to question such testimonies, our naturalistically trained minds, when confronted with such accounts make us demand that the teller "prove it." I cannot. All I can tell you is that life for me changed that day—religion suffered a fatal wound. It would die slowly and unwillingly, gasping for every lie it had breathed into me disguised as "life". The Life had conquered life. Jesus was truly alive; and my journey to Life had entered the Way and the End. Love had found me; and I had fallen in love with Jesus.

But I had questions—and they came immediately. As I lay weeping in Joy I asked, "God, why? What is going on? What has changed?" I went to God's Word to listen and search for a reason. The Lord quietly took me to the book of John, chapter 14, verse 21, "He who has My commandments and keeps them is the one who loves Me; and he who loves Me will be loved by My Father, and I will love him and will disclose Myself to him."

"I will disclose myself to him." The word "disclose" means to make apparent, or become known on an intimate basis. This was certainly what had begun in my life. Jesus and Father were suddenly real. And my cold heart had melted into their eternal love. So, the love described and the disclosure described rang true with the words of this verse. But I protested, "But, Lord, I've had your commandments for a long time."

His immediate answer was, "No. I did not say he who has a copy of my commandments, but rather 'he who has my commandments.' My commandments are now part of you. Where you go they go; where you are they are; they are in you. You have them."

But I knew I had Him on the other part of the verse. My protest continued, "But, Father, you know I can't keep your commandments. I fail and always have!" He did not answer me at that time. I was allowed to have a two-week argument about keeping God's commandments. I say I was allowed, because it was a one sided argument. Father just listened and did not answer. But the answer was coming.

One day on my lunch break I was sitting in my office at work, with my Bible opened to John 14, and continuing my monolog with God. (It was another one of those times I was glad the door was closed and no one was with me, as I was literally pounding on my desk and in speaking in a frustrated manner to apparently no one.) I was repeating, "God, you know I can't keep your commandments!!!" And He suddenly spoke, "Stop it. You are looking at the word completely wrong. When you go home tonight, the first thing you do is to look up the word 'keep'." I finished my workday and headed home in anticipation of what I did not know. Upon my arrival, I greeted my wife and headed straight for the Greek dictionaries. I was about to have one of the most shocking revelations of my life.

Chapter 5
Keep My Commandments

Religion has trained us well. We have the capacity to look directly at truth, and to redefine the words which convey that truth into meaningless rhetoric; thereby creating an illogical God whose good news is not good, and whose frightening favor must be somehow sought by creating and performing deeds which one cannot create or perform. Defining terms Biblically is too much trouble and to be left to the professionals. Let them tell us what to think—a rather amazing approach to one's fate for eternity. It is far too often true that most of us simply "never thought about it."

As stated earlier, my life had been busy—taking care of those obligations which, I had come to believe, would make me approved of by God. And that also meant obedience to God. In today's theology that means whatever I "feel" is right. There is no true standard of behavior as we are no longer "under the law." Or so I was told. My beliefs "in God" were about to die.

The entrance to my office that day was the exit to my way of life.

"He who has my commandments and keeps them, he it is who loves me." The Lord had clarified the statement, "he who has my commandments" as "placing them in your life, coming into your possession." But "keeps them"?! Honestly, it was so daunting a prospect that I simply read it in Scripture—and ignored it. And now I was under orders to research what I already knew—I was to obey His commandments.

I certainly was going to obey His current commandment and went quickly to Strong's Concordance Dictionary. The Strong's number is 5083 and the word is transliterated *tereo*. It is defined here as "to watch; to guard (from loss or injury by keeping the eye upon); hold fast." Further, according to Dr. Spiros Zodhiates in his <u>Complete Word Study Bible and Reference CD</u>, the word means, "to watch, observe attentively, keep the eyes fixed upon, guard a prisoner." My first thought upon reading or hearing the word "keep" with reference to God's commandments is what most of us think, because it is what we have been taught—I think "obey." Yet, the above references are clear; it is <u>only figuratively</u> that the word is translated "obey." In other words, **we made up that part of the definition**—it is <u>not</u> the correct interpretation or definition of the word "keep." The same word is used in the Greek text for those watching Jesus on the cross, Peter being kept in prison, the guards on Jesus' tomb, and keeping back the best wine for last at the wedding at Cana. The <u>New</u> <u>International</u> <u>Version</u> does translate the word as "obey," but this is not correct and is only in keeping with the inference mankind has made upon the word. My religious and self-exalting interpretation of "keep" is "I must obey."

And it has been so historically. While I was attending a worship service one Sunday morning, two women were announcing the latest children's program for the congregation. It was to be on the Ten Commandments. The room was filled with almost 500 professing believers, mostly adults. One of the women asked, "How many of you know the Ten Commandments?" I do not know the feelings of others as not one hand went up, but I was ashamed. I had been challenged years before to memorize the Ten Commandments, but had resisted as I had been taught that the Law did not apply to me because I was a "Christian." I purposed to memorize them and meditate upon them.

I had often read the Psalms and worried about David when he wrote "how I love thy law." I wondered, if while practicing with his sling, David had not come a little too close to his own head with the stones. God's law was so dry to me, so lifeless. But that was because I had not meditated on it as David had. My fellowship with the Lord grew deeper and deeper (just as He had promised). Now I loved God's Law! Now I delighted in His Law! And He continued to show me His ways and grew closer and more powerful in living His life in mine as my belief system began to agree with His truth and righteousness.

And the next shock was on the way.

While meditating on the second commandment one evening I came to the phrase, "for I, the LORD your God, am a jealous God, visiting the iniquity of the fathers on the children, on the third and the fourth generations of those who hate Me, but showing loving kindness to thousands, to those who love Me and keep My commandments." I froze. "Love me and keep my commandments." In usual fashion, I began to argue, "But Lord, this is Hebrew, not Greek!"—a fact I was sure had escaped the author. His reply was, "I have been bringing you to this point for 40 years. Get up and look up the word." I obeyed. The word is transliterated "*shamar*" and is defined as "to hedge around something, to keep, guard, protect, observe, attend", precisely the same meaning as the Greek—and again, our interpretation of the word as "obey," only a human intimation.

Think how silly it would be, if we redefined the word "keep" in our every day language as we have done to God's Word. If I asked you to keep my writing pen for me, would you obey the pen? If I asked a friend to keep my children would that friend watch over and guard them carefully or obey them? The possessions which you have that are most precious to you—do you guard them and watch over them as the treasure they are, or do you offer obedience?

Please understand I am certainly not speaking against obedience of God's Word and Law!!! Scripture is full of references regarding obeying God. He is Creator and Lord and is therefore to be obeyed. I am speaking here of something much deeper than our simple concept of obedience. Keeping God's commandments "guarded, observed intently, one's eyes fixed upon them" does require obedience. But the obedience God is requiring is exactly that—to keep the commandments before my eyes. Man says obey His commandments. God says guard, observe intently, and fix your eyes upon His commandments. What He means is to look at them, think on them, hold them close, speak them to your self, sit and listen to them, speak them back to God—in short, what the Bible means when it speaks of meditation on His Word.

And this takes us back to the previous discussion on double-mindedness and man's belief system. According to Scripture there is a seat of belief, a deep place where true belief grows and exists which affects our lives and behaviors. It is called the "heart." A thorough discussion of the concept of the heart would be a book in itself, but looking at just a few verses of Scripture will certainly give us insight on the matter:

> Deut. 6:4 Hear, O Israel: The LORD our God is one LORD:
> 5 And thou shalt love the LORD thy God with all thine **heart**, and with all thy soul, and with all thy might.
> 6 And **these words**, which I command thee this day, **shall be in thine heart**:

Deut. 11:18 Therefore shall ye **lay up these my words in your heart** and in your soul, and bind them for a sign upon your hand, that they may be as frontlets between your eyes.

Ps. 14:1 The fool hath **said in his heart**, There is no God. They are corrupt, they have done abominable works, there is none that doeth good.

Ps. 40:8 **I delight to do thy will, O my God: yea, thy law is within my heart.**

Ps. 49:3 My mouth shall speak of wisdom; and the meditation of my **heart** shall be of **understanding**.

Ps. 119:112 I have **inclined mine heart to perform** thy statutes alway, even unto the end.

Prov. 2:10 When **wisdom entereth into thine heart**, and knowledge is pleasant unto thy soul;
11 Discretion shall preserve thee, understanding shall keep thee:

Romans 6:17 "But God be thanked, that ye were the servants of sin,
but ye have **obeyed from the heart** that form of doctrine which was delivered you."

Romans 10:10 "For **with the heart man believeth unto righteousness**; and with the mouth confession is made unto salvation. For the scripture saith, whosoever believeth on him shall not be ashamed."

Eph. 6:5 Servants, be obedient to them that are your masters according to the flesh, with fear and trembling, in singleness of your heart, as unto Christ; not with eye service, as men pleasers; but as the servants of Christ, **doing the will of God from the heart**;

HEB 3:12 Take heed, brethren, lest there be in any of you **an evil heart of unbelief**, in departing from the living God.

We can see from these verses that we believe things in our heart and that belief produces our behaviors. That must be repeated: <u>We believe something in our heart and that belief produces behavior</u>. And it is from meditation that the heart believes. But meditation must not be thought of in terms of emptying the mind or of chanting a mantra to one's self or of a turning of the mind to contemplate religious thoughts. Meditation is in some ways just thinking. It is thinking on a particular subject and thinking on it often. It is using the imagination to think on the subject. It is specifically ruminating on words or actions relating to that subject. When I hear something enough times or think on something often enough, it becomes belief in my heart. And it is the belief in my heart that becomes action.

There are many highly intelligent people who know intellectually that using tobacco is harmful to one's health. They know that fact in their brain. But they continue to use tobacco. Logically this makes no sense—unless one acknowledges that we have a seat of belief that drives behaviors which is not the intellect. The intellect knows that tobacco use will adversely affect my health—yet I continue to use tobacco. Somewhere in me is a belief that overrides the intellect. It is a belief that I often come to without fully knowing that I believe it, but from continued and often subtle meditation on that belief, it becomes "truth" in my heart and I behave in accordance with that belief. In the case of tobacco it may be that I have come to believe that such diseases happen to "those other people" but not to me. This is reinforced for many years by the insidiousness of the disease process and the outward appearance of health. The belief may be established from watching and then mimicking behavior of parents or friends who appear unaffected by their participation in the behavior. Or perhaps the belief that tobacco use makes me more socially acceptable is a more powerful desire than the desire to preserve my health. Or the person may have a belief that his or her life has little value and that belief overrides any health concerns one may have. Note that none of these examples of deep seated beliefs are logical or in keeping with known science or fact. But they are of such strength that I bet my life on their truth. I came to believe these "truths" over time—a repeated exposure and meditation on the lies that it will not affect me, it did not affect them, or that I am worthless. These thoughts become my meditation, which eventually overrides fact and becomes my behavior, and in this case and many others, eventually may become my death. Biologically you are what you eat; soulishly and behaviorally you are what you meditate.

Chapter 6
The Old New Covenant

"He who has my commandments and keeps them, he it is who loves me…" I have heard those who say that this verse is speaking of the proof that someone loves Jesus. If one has and keeps Jesus' commandments, it is the outward proof of love for Jesus. And they are correct. But it is also a way of being. It is having His commandments and keeping them that loves Jesus. I John 4:19 states "We love, because He first loved us." Therefore, it is God's love for us that comes first. It compels us, empowers us to love Him. But He defines that loving with the keeping of His word.

This, of course, is exactly the way relationships function. Attraction to a person is naturally followed by a desire to know about his mind. And we gain that knowledge by hearing his words. As the relationship deepens, time with him and his words proves them true or false and if true, trust develops; not because we know about him, but because we know him. Why should we then question and wonder that God would tell us to abide, to live in His Word, and let it "richly dwell within" us? Or should it stagger our imaginations when the story of the Messiah of mankind opens with the statement, "In the beginning was the Word…and the Word was God"? Certainly, God is supernatural. But He must bring that supernatural life to our natural lives. Something must explain Him. It cannot be my imagination, or my religious desires creating a god in my own image. That will and must bring about hatred and war when I think others disagree with my religion or denomination. The explanation of God must come from God, which He has given us in His written Word (the hearing) and in His living Word (the knowing).

The final goal of a relationship is not knowing facts about the person. Knowing facts is not "knowing" the person. God will bring insights into His Word as I meditate and seek Him. But <u>the purpose of meditation, Bible study, or prayer—the whole of Christian action—is not insights; it is intimacy</u>. Even God's constant complaint about sin is that it separates me from Him.

Jesus' prayer before Gethsemane recorded in John 17 was for our union with one another through our union with Him. Look at His definition of eternal life in verse 3, "This is eternal life that they may know you, the only true God, and Jesus Christ whom you have sent." Jesus defines eternal life, not in terms of heaven or future or mansions, but in knowing God and in knowing Himself. (He also stated in a rarely referenced verse in Matthew 19:17, "but if you wish to enter into life, <u>keep</u> the commandments.") The Greek word for "know" in verse 3 is *"ginosko"*. According to Dr. Spiros Zodhiates it means "to know in a beginning or completed sense." It is the same word used by Jesus when speaking of our left hand not knowing what the right does, and of sexual relations between Joseph and Mary in Matthew 1:25, "he knew her not." This is not a shallow "knowing," but a knowing of the deepest intimacy. Eternal life is not just a living forever, it is life now and forever, but only because of an intimate knowing of Father and Son. Continuing in John 17 we see in verses 21 and 23 the reason for His prayer: "that they all may be one; even as you, Father, are in Me and I in You, that they may also be in Us, so that the world may believe that you sent Me...I in them and You in Me, that they may be perfected in unity, so that the world may know that You sent Me, and loved them, even as You have loved Me." Here Jesus again repeats His prayer to Father that believers are to have deep relationship with God, to the point of being "in" Father and Son. The purpose of that intimacy is that the world would believe. If those words are true, is it any wonder that the world's response when looking at those proclaiming to be disciples of Christ, see only another religion, and do not believe. Again, the Christian religion is no better than any other of the world's religions. It was never designed to be so, as evidenced in our continually failing evangelistic efforts. Relationship turned into a religion is simply unbelievable.

⟋ Much has been made regarding "experiential religion." The fear is, and rightfully so, that some will base their belief and their faith in God on an experience they have had or for which they are looking. Such a faith is not a Biblical faith, but an imaginary faith, built upon the shifting sands of feelings and sensation which must change and must fail. But in the concern that experience or emotion not be a basis for faith we cannot ignore the fact that we as persons "experience" life. Without "experience," life loses its real-ness. God gave us emotions and senses—the tools to "experience." They inherently cannot be purposeless. They do not give us purpose or lead us in purpose, but they have purpose. Life is experienced. Knowledge is gained from experience. Learning itself is experienced. Experience and emotion are not knowledge, nor should they be the guiding light of direction in life. It is true that many through the ages have turned away from the Word of God as the standard of truth and have replaced it with experience and pragmatism, seeking a god made in man's image whose purpose is to tickle one's ears and tickle one's fancy. Religion is man made, whether experiential or with whitewashed gravestones of "God-controlling" theologies.

Again, God's purpose in Christianity is not religion, but a relationship with a people called to be His own.

Relationships survive within frameworks of rules and mores, and violation of these will cause great destruction to any relationship. But within those frameworks, relationship is "experienced," making the relationship real. If a relationship is faked or not real, it is not desirable. Of course, if one continues to believe that Christianity is simply a religion, little I have to say will matter. But for those who see that our religion is a vain, worthless thing to a God, whose purpose in all things appears to be love, please hear me. Perhaps the judgment against experiential religion is founded and correct. But to state that a relationship with God should not be experienced is false.

This is actually all through the Bible, but we have been blinded by the light of theology and religion. Once my religious mindset has been removed, the entire Bible reads quite a bit differently. We could go almost anywhere in Scripture to prove this point, but let us use something which should be familiar to all New Testament believers—the New Covenant.

The stipulations and major points of the New Covenant are listed in Jeremiah 31:33-34:

> "But this is the covenant which I will make with the house of Israel
>
> after those days," declares the LORD, "I will put My law within them and on their heart I will write it; and I will be their God, and they shall be My people. They will not teach again, each man his neighbor and each man his brother, saying, 'Know the LORD,' for they will all know Me, from the least of them to the greatest of them," declares the LORD, "for I will forgive their iniquity, and their sin I will remember no more."

These are repeated in the New Testament in the 8th chapter of Hebrews.

There are four main points to the New Covenant:
1. I will put My law within them and on their heart I will write it.
2. I will be their God and they shall be my people.
3. They will not teach 'know the Lord' for all will know Me.
4. I will forgive their iniquity and their sin I will remember no more.

We do not have space to dwell on all of the incredible life-giving facets of the New Covenant. The Apostle Paul and others have already done much of that work in the Greek Scriptures of the New Testament. Even with that, believers remain sadly ignorant of the covenant given to them by Father. We have tended to focus on one part of the covenant—that of forgiveness of sin. While this is obviously important, it is not the goal or major point of the New Covenant. Scripture speaks much of sin. Forgiveness of sin is a requirement for the covenant to work, but few of us know why. Many of us believe God is angry and just wants us to behave. But that is not the reason God hates sin. God hates sin because He loves us and wants relationship with us. Here are just a few of the scriptures showing this truth:

Isaiah 59:1 Behold, the LORD'S hand is not so short That it cannot
save; Nor is His ear so dull That it cannot hear.
2 But your iniquities have made a **separation** between you and your
God, And your sins have hidden His face from you so that He does not hear.

Jeremiah 5:23 'But this people has a stubborn and rebellious heart; they have turned aside and departed 24 'they do not say in their heart, "Let us now fear the LORD our God, Who gives rain in its season, both the autumn rain and the spring rain, Who keeps for us The appointed weeks of the harvest."
25 'Your iniquities have turned these away, and your sins have **withheld good** from you.

Acts 3:18 "But the things which God announced beforehand by the mouth of all the prophets, that His Christ would suffer, He has thus fulfilled.
19 "Therefore repent and return, so that your sins may be wiped away, in order that times of refreshing may come from the **presence** of the Lord;
[emphasis added]

God's main complaint about sin and iniquity is that it separates us from Him. It takes us away from His loving protection and makes us the slave of self and sin. His jealousy for us does not take the form of our trite, self-centered human jealousy; God's jealousy is a jealousy that knows our "lovers" will destroy our lives and that relationship with "The Life" is our only escape from the death that is life in and for me. Sin causes suffering; the wages of sin is death. But Scripture is very clear; Father doesn't kill us—we choose death rather than life. Jesus said to _know_ Him and to _know_ Father is eternal life. No where in Scripture do we see that a religion based on Jesus or on Yahweh brings eternal life—which brings us again to the New Covenant.

✓ Most Christians know and accept only one part of the covenant—forgiveness of sins. But that is only step one, the first step into the covenant.

We have been invited to the most sumptuous banquet to which one can be invited. But we have stepped just inside the door and stopped, congratulating ourselves on having arrived and attended. We never enter the banquet hall, we never eat of the meal, we never speak to our Honored Host. Christ suffered for us and died for us, tearing the veil that separated us from entering into the life of God. That veil was sin. Jesus became that veil—He became sin for us. His flesh was torn, His body broken that we, being made part of that body by the New Covenant, may enter into the presence of God the Father. But there is much more than just "entering in" by forgiveness of sin and iniquity. We have not entered into a religious covenant; covenants are between friends. Friendship is not about religion. And the New Covenant is about experiential relationship.

Note the first part of the covenant: "I will write My law within them." We have already seen that keeping God's commandments is equated with loving Him. The Law of God is no longer on the outside for the obeying; it is inside for the keeping. God puts it there. This is not about religious dos and don'ts; it is about loving God with God supplying all the requirements for that love. The covenant then states, "I will be their God and they will be My people." This is possession on both sides; God possessing me, my possessing God. And finally, God states they will all "know" Me, from the least to the greatest. The Hebrew word for "know" here is *yadha.* Its definition includes knowing, to be acquainted with, to know by experience, and to discover. It is the same word used in Genesis 4:1 which states that Adam "knew his wife; and she conceived." This word does not imply a flippant knowledge of facts, but of understanding, knowing, and intimacy on the deepest level.

The point is that the New Covenant (Biblical Christianity) was never meant to be a new religion. All aspects of it point to one thing—a deep, personal relationship with the very God of creation. Forgiveness of sin is to do away with separation; writing the Law on one's heart is the path to loving God; God and I will be one another's possession; and I will deeply, experientially know God, the Father. No amount of twisting Scripture to fit religion, no amount of theologizing will change this fact. God wants relationship with me; He wants relationship with you. He gave His greatest love to get my love.

And do not think that the Old Testament was not based on faith and relationship. Abraham was called the "friend of God." Enoch walked with God, and God took him to be with Him. Moses talked with God as a friend, face to face. David's heart of love and relationship with God are poured out in the Psalms. And the New Covenant is actually quite old—older than all the other covenants of Scripture. Revelation 13:8 states, "And all that dwell upon the earth shall worship him [the beast], whose names are not written in the book of life of the Lamb slain from the foundation of the world."

Chapter 7
The Great Omission

The disciples experienced Jesus, physically, emotionally, logically, and spiritually. He wants no less for us. Paul speaks of "having a desire to depart and to be with Christ, which is far better" and of "seeing through a glass darkly but then face to face." Obviously he is speaking of the future and the eternal state of being with Christ without the confines and limitations on "knowing" caused by our flesh. But it is also clear that Paul and other disciples knew and experienced Christ—after His death and ascension, in this life. Stephen "saw" Jesus, Paul "heard" Jesus, John was "in the spirit" for Revelation, and the people spoken of in Acts experienced Jesus. It is not just in a future estate that disciples are to know God intimately.

In Matthew 28 Jesus gives us the words which have come to be known as the Great Commission. The church has historically viewed these words as "marching orders"; and that they may be. But orders followed precisely will be of little good if they are interpreted to mean something different than the commander communicated. Often our evangelical fervor has led us to move forward in the name of Christ, when we were actually acting in the name of "Me," Power, or The Church. Even a short study of church history will show this to be true as we see cult after cult, church-run states, the Crusades, and false doctrines gleaned from the Bible to control the masses by fear.

The verses in Matthew 28 would seem to be forthright: "And Jesus came and spake unto them, saying, All power is given unto me in heaven and in earth. Go ye therefore, and teach all nations, baptizing them in the name of the Father, and of the Son, and of the Holy Ghost:

Teaching them to observe all things whatsoever I have commanded you: and, lo, I am with you alway, even unto the end of the world." (King James Version) "All power" given to Christ is readily understood. The command to "Go" is sharp enough to cause little disagreement. The next phrase is translated here as "<u>teach</u> all nations," and a few lines later we see "<u>teaching</u> them to observe." So twice we see the word "<u>teach</u>." But the two words are not the same Greek word. The phrase "teach all nations" would be more accurately translated "disciple all nations." There is a difference.

Teaching whether defined in Greek or English is instruction, usually by mouth. It certainly is part of discipleship. But our concern as Christians must not be for man's definition of spiritual matters, but Christ's. The very word "Christian" means "of Christ" or "like Christ." If we are to be disciples of Christ, it behooves us to define "disciple" as He defines "disciple." Jesus does not define disciple as "convert." In fact, no where in Scripture are we told to make converts. Yet this is what many have done with the "Great Commission." We argue with nonbelievers, which is un-Biblical. We use manipulative programs to lure nonbelievers, which is un-Biblical. We chalk up another number as being "saved" when they recite the "sinner's prayer," which is not in the Bible.

Wringing our hands in anguish and confusion we look with wonder at the destruction of society around us and the lack of Biblical belief seen in the church, as each succeeding generation slides further and further into the pit of self. Exhausted we fall with relief into the waiting, anesthetic arms of the next busy-church program, guaranteed to bring new life and new numbers to "your church." We do not see disciples of Christ because we are not making disciples of

Christ. Our seminaries are more concerned with disseminating the doctrinal dogma of their denomination or arguing the merits of theoretical theologies than concerned over making disciples for Christ.

✎ The Great Commission has become the Great Omission. Again, the main reason for this is our non-Biblical world view. The church currently has a man-centered world view, placing man at the center of all time and purpose, and elevating the "church" to the position of a god to be served, sacrificed to, and sought after.

But what is the Biblical view of a disciple of Jesus Christ? Scripture gives us a number of characteristics of a disciple, but only one definition. In evangelical meetings we often use John 8:32 to encourage others to come to faith in Christ: "you shall know the truth, and the truth will set you free." This phrase is even written in the stone of a building on one of the largest secular universities in the United States. But the way that it is used in both places is just that, a phrase, an incomplete phrase, and therefore not communicating fully what the speaker was saying. For the complete verse is as follows, "So Jesus was saying to those Jews who had believed Him, 'If you continue in My word, then you are truly disciples of Mine; and you will know the truth, and the truth will make you free.'"

Notice that it says Jesus was speaking to those who had already "believed Him." By the end of the chapter, these *believers* accused Jesus of being illigetimate, of being demonized, and finally attempted to murder Him. The ensuing conversation is one of the most intense in scripture, with Jesus drawing the dividing line between Himself and his audience—that of "keeping" God's word.

And that dividing line is where Jesus separates someone who is a "believer" from a "disciple." And, as already shown, what a dividing line it is. We have churches and history fraught with believers, but so few disciples. We train people to "only believe"; but without a Biblical standard of truth, we mostly "make-believe." There is no change in behavior, no hunger for God, no relationship with Him, and no power or witness which proclaims Christ's life in them to others. One of the main reasons for this is that we have defined "believing in God" as belief in His existence, rather than belief in His character. We have exchanged belief in Him as the personal God for a false belief in a benevolent (but angry), far removed entity in the sky. Just as we cannot trust or believe in someone whose words and character are unknown by us, we cannot believe God because His Words and character are unknown to us. Scripture states that Abraham, the father of our faith, *believed God and it was reckoned to him as righteousness.* It does not say he believed *in God.* Abraham, the friend of God, displayed a much more personal faith than the sanitized, unemployed God we have created in our own image. His faith was a far cry from our evangelical mantras which encourage people to "say the magic words, believe real hard, and you too can go to heaven."

This in no way is an argument against an evangelistic sharing of the gospel. But it is a statement that the gospel which many are sharing is a false, Unbiblical fairy tale which blurs the true rightful claim of lordship and kingship of Christ over a life by substituting for it a cathartic confession. We are commanded to make disciples. A disciple is not a convert or a confessor. A disciple is one who continues in or abides in the Word of Christ. Disciple is never defined in scripture in any other way.

As long as we insist on redefining God's Words and ways, we will continue to fail to see true expansion of the kingdom of God. As long as we insist on coerced confessions rather than living disciples, our churches and families will continue to be powerless in the face of the secularization of society. As long as we allow creeds and theologies to shape our lives and our God rather than our feeding on His word, we will remain spiritual emaciates. If we would return to making disciples of Christ, rather than converts, evangelism would take care of itself. The world would sit up and take notice because of the radical changes they would see in Christian lives. And Christians would so love their Lord that evangelism would not be a contrived program, but a very natural conversation.

When we expect the life of Christ to be produced in others through man's illegitimate methods, are we any different than the believers mentioned above who called Jesus a product of man's illegitimacy?

In John 8:51 Jesus said "if anyone keeps My Word he shall never see death." The believers' retort was that Christ was possessed by a demon. How are we different when we falsely promise eternal life for temporal confession?

Jesus stated in verse 37 of the same chapter to this same group of believers that their wish to kill him was because *His Word had no place in them*. How are we less guilty of murder than they when we seek conversions through the word of man rather than making disciples of Christ through the Word of God?

It is a certain fact that knowing the truth sets us free. But knowing the truth comes by abiding in the word of Jesus Christ, and thereby becoming His disciple. Only when I am a disciple, will I be able to make a disciple. And only when I have been made free from the power of the Word and the Son, will I be able to witness to that fact—and invite others to follow.

Chapter 8
The Wonderful Counselor's Counsel

"So Jesus was saying to those Jews who had believed Him, "If you continue in My word, then you are truly disciples of Mine; and you will know the truth, and the truth will make you free." As believers in the Lord Jesus Christ, we do not have the choice on whether to believe these words or not. If I do not believe His words, I don't believe Him. How can I believe a person and yet simultaneously not believe that person? Either you are a believer or you are not a believer. It sounds trite, but a believer is someone who believes. If Jesus said something, and I claim to be a "believer," I am to act in accordance with my statement and believe Him. No amount of theological twisting and turning can change that fact.

And here Jesus tells us something we must believe: continuing in His word not only makes us His disciples but makes us know the truth, and knowing truth makes us free. Truth has always been under attack. From the Garden of Eden to the foretold end of the current world system, the attack remains the steady, hypnotic mantra that God has deceived man and has not spoken truth. And man has believed the lie rather than believe God. Man's heart truly is full of lies. Man's very nature is not that of the heavenly Father but of the one to whom he bowed the knee and to whom he gave authority in the Garden of Eden. And as this nature is one with the father of lies, it is quite easy to agree with lies. Jesus stated this lostness of man when he said in Matthew 5 "[I]f the light that is in you is darkness, how great is that darkness." In other words, when one believes lies as truth, truth cannot be perceived as truth; truth will be perceived as a lie. The lie will be acted on and followed as a way of life.⤷ Real belief in something results in action, because that belief is actually part of the life. We act because we *believe* something will benefit others or us. If we do not believe there is benefit in action we will not act; which brings us to the definition of "truth" itself.

The false philosophy of relativism has become firmly established in our modern thinking—not that it is modern thinking for the concept is quite old. One of its major tenets is that truth is relative, or, stated as it is most often heard, "Something may be truth for you, but not truth for me." In a warped way this is true—if one defines truth as what one believes. Those who state that "the only absolute truth is that there are no absolutes" are simply stating they have settled on an acceptable excuse to use others to the fullest extent of their selfishness and evil. And, while we have already established that we do act on what we believe to be true, it is not true that everything one believes is true. In other words, we can believe and act on things that are false. In fact, most of what we do every day is more reflexive than thoughtful, simply a response to stimuli from an unquestioned and unseen belief system. And, if that unseen belief system is not true, we will act in ways not in accord with truth and with the ways of God. At the crucifixion of Christ, Pilate asked him a popular question: "What is truth?"—a question which comes through the arrogance of man by un-defining the defining of "define," and through that, believing he has come to wisdom. If truth is relative, there is no truth, and, as such, no reality or statements regarding that reality.

Webster's Dictionary defines truth as ", conformity with fact or reality." Jesus defined truth in two ways, both on a very personal level. He first defined truth as Himself personally in John 15, "I am...the truth." His very life, all that is Jesus—on personal, biological, spiritual, verbal, and mental levels—all is truth. Nothing of falsehood exists in him. Nothing incompatible with truth exists in Him. In other words, all in Jesus is fully compatible and only compatible with fact or reality. All beliefs outside of the personhood of Jesus are not compatible with fact or reality. With that statement, it must be stated that creation itself is compatible with Jesus and, therefore, compatible with fact and reality. All creation was created through Him and for Him. All true science and knowledge is compatible with Jesus. And here we come to Jesus' second definition of truth. In John 17:17 He prays to Father, "Sanctify them in the truth; Your word is truth." The Word of God is truth. Therefore, all beliefs outside of the word of God are not compatible with fact or reality. And these two definitions of truth are fully compatible with one another, for in John 1:14 we read, "[A]nd the Word became flesh and dwelt among us, and we saw His glory, glory as of the only begotten from the Father, full of grace and truth." Jesus is the Word of God; Jesus is truth.

"If you continue in My word, then you are truly disciples of Mine; and you will know the truth, and the truth will make you free." Continuing in God's Word makes one know the truth—Jesus. And again, here we have simply another way of stating that listening to the words of Christ builds a relationship with Him, it makes us know Him, the Truth. Continuing, or abiding, as it is stated in other translations, in Jesus' words makes us intimate with Him. But, as stated earlier, this intimacy changes my life. Abiding in His word, develops such a deep relationship with Him that His very life comes to live in me. That life changes my life—forever. "This is eternal life, that they may know You, the only true God, and Jesus Christ whom You have sent." (John 17:3) Eternal life is knowing God and Jesus Christ.

And knowing comes from abiding in His word—but this knowing is different than any other knowing. This knowing sets one free.

Freedom is something of which the world dreams but rarely defines and even more rarely experiences. It is most often mentioned in the political realm with the desire for a people, race, or nation to be free. But freedom of any type always involves responsibility. True freedom is never freedom to do all of one's wishes. True freedom must always be restricted by law. Mankind, in his current state will not govern himself. Total freedom results in total depravity. Man without law to restrict his behavior becomes the measure of behavior on an individual level—which is the problem. Man is not God and never will be. My personal selfishness and lusts (defined by myself as "freedom") will inevitably overrule another's personal selfishness and lusts, thereby restricting that person's freedom. The oft repeated question, "Why can't we all just get along?" is worth answering. But the answer does not come on a societal level. Nor is the answer a statement. The most accurate answer to that question is another question, "Why can't I get along?" For the answer to man's wars, slaveries, murders, and holocausts are not plural—it is the problem in the individual. My individual desires drive me to use others for my good, which must clash with their good. Without restrictions to his freedom, man has consistently displayed the wild, uncivilized, savage beast that he is. The evolutionary rules of "survival of the fittest" and "the ascent of mankind" must involve judgment of fitness and who has ascended and who has not, which begs the question ",Who is fit to judge fitness for survival?" And, when that judgment is made, the response is not freedom but murder, war, and genocide—the history of mankind.

And the history of mankind and our inability to rule ourselves will be repeated continually until the history of man, the individual, is changed by man, the individual, receiving the ability to rule self. True salvation is not just salvation from sin—it is salvation from self. And, if I have been saved from myself, mankind has been saved from me. The personhood of Jesus, the Truth, offers me freedom as I know Him; as I have relationship with Him He gives me freedom from self. Only Truth personified, living in the individual man, can bring personal freedom. And only personal freedom for man, the individual, can produce freedom for man, the species.

True freedom is the absence of fear. Fear is the main driving force behind most of the goals in human life. I walk in fear of pain, fear of love, fear of abandonment, fear of hunger, thirst, death, injury, the future, the past, today, lack, missing out, wrong decisions, and even fear itself. I recently heard a person, who frequently participates in daredevil stunts just for the thrill of doing so, say repeatedly, "I will not let fear keep me from doing the things I dream of doing." I must salute his spirit and his desire to look fear in the face. On the other hand he missed something—his driving force of the fear of missing out on not doing something he desires to do. Just as it is true that truth sets us free, it is non-truth (lies) that brings us bondage. Hebrews 2:14-15 states, "Therefore, since the children share in flesh and blood, He Himself likewise also partook of the same, that through death He might render powerless him who had the power of death, that is, the devil, and might free those who through fear of death were subject to slavery all their lives." True freedom is the absence of fear; and the absence of fear is peace. Freedom and peace are two of the main goals in the human life. And when we lack these we will naturally try to move toward the fulfillment of them in our lives, and that fulfillment is often by seeking guidance through counselors.

Counsel is often needed from time to time. But what often is being passed off as counsel is more in line with II Timothy 4:3-4 "For the time will come when they will not endure sound doctrine; but wanting to have their ears tickled, they will accumulate for themselves teachers in accordance to their own desires, and will turn away their ears from the truth and will turn aside to myths." Counsel is often not based on the truths of God's word ("sound doctrine"), but rather the tenets of secular, pragmatic psychological principles which may "work" in accordance with the goals of the parties involved. The goals and means of counsel for the believer must be in accordance with the Kingdom of God—not the interests of man. In Matthew 16, Jesus begins to show His disciples that He is going to be crucified. Peter takes Jesus aside and begins to give him his counsel. Jesus' reply speaks volumes to man centered counsel: "But He turned and said to Peter, 'Get behind Me, Satan! You are a stumbling block to Me; for you are not setting your mind on God's interests, but man's.'" Man's interests are usually on his comfort. One does not seek a counselor when things are going well. A counselor is sought in time of need. But if the counselor is focused on repairing the lack of comfort in the counselee and the counselee is focused on the same, the interests of man will outweigh the interests of God; and the counsel given will not be on the furtherance of the Kingdom in either life, but rather achieving the goal of man's pleasure and comfort. Not that God does not desire comfort for His people. He does. The familiar verse of Isaiah 40:1 states, "Comfort ye, comfort ye my people, saith your God." But this verse must be placed in its context. Further reading of the passage brings out the following statements: "[H]er iniquity has been removed, that she has received of the Lord's hand double for all her sins...Clear the way for the Lord...make smooth in the desert a highway for our God...the glory of the Lord will be revealed...All flesh is grass...surely the people are grass. The grass withers, the flower fades, but the word of our God stands forever." The purpose of the passage is that the people of God receive comfort, but before that comfort first is discomfort for sin and iniquity with the purpose of that discomfort to encourage the people to return to God's Kingship in God's way.

God often uses man's discomfort to bring him to truth and life. Pain and suffering have a singular effect on the lack of humility in man. C. S. Lewis has stated that pain is God's megaphone to rouse a deaf world. Jesus Christ stated to seek *first* His Kingdom and His righteousness, not my kingdom nor my comfort. God's creation and creatures are governed by His laws. When one crosses the barriers of these laws, pain or damage is a result. All of creation is set up on a cause and effect basis. If God's intent is that we seek Him first, and suffering is one of His tools for directing us in that way, it would seem logical to conclude that God's purpose in suffering is not for us to discover a way to relieve that suffering apart from seeking Him.

A phrase often heard today is "quality of life." While this has the sound of wisdom, it is the exact opposite of the ways of God. My focus should be on a "life of quality" rather than "quality of life." Jesus said in Matthew 16:25, "For whoever wishes to save his life will lose it; but whoever loses his life for My sake will find it." Jesus cuts to the very heart of the matter. And it does not matter what matter may be the subject. My seeking my own way, me seeking to fulfill my life with life, is an eternal death. Seeking to fulfill my life is an endless, restless race which is never won, one in which I must ever keep one step in a new, contrived, senseless fad which will cover that emptiness and loneliness which is "Me;" for to stop my frantic race would find me locked in an eternal stare at the one object I cannot face—The Peaceless Me. James 1:12 states, "Blessed is a man who perseveres under trial; for once he has been approved, he will receive the crown of life which the Lord has promised to those who love Him." The life spoken of here is not a future, eternal life. It is life now. For either I will rule life—or life will rule me. And the rulership of life is granted by the King of Life, not to those individuals whose passion is their own passions, but those who "persevere under trial."

Most of us believe we make decisions logically. And that is probably true. But logic requires presuppositions (a basic belief system) upon which decisions are based. A simple, example would be crossing a bridge over a river. If I am driving, my behavior is simply driving in a forward direction with few thoughts about bridge structure and engineering. I do not consider the presuppositions regarding whether the bridge will hold me or if it fully spans the river. These facts are assumed to be true and are a part of my belief system which I act upon without considering each bridge to which I come. Another word to describe these presuppositions would be faith. I simply believe the bridge is there and is strong and will hold me. So our behaviors, whether toward God or not, are behaviors of faith. This is verified in Hebrews 11:1, one of the most famous verses on faith: "Now faith is the substance of things hoped for, the evidence of things not seen." According to Dr. Spiros Zodhiates in the <u>Complete Word Study Bible CD</u>, the Greek word translated "substance" means literally "that which <u>underlies</u> the apparent" and the word translated "evidence" literally means "not merely the charge on the basis of which one is convicted, but the manifestation of the truth of that charge and the results to be reaped." So, we could easily say that "faith is that which underlies the apparent (seen) hope, the manifestation of truth not seen." How is hope (an inward belief) apparent and how is truth manifested? Hope, faith, and truth are seen, not by feelings or by trumped up excitement but by outward, daily, natural behavior. As stated earlier, my belief system is seen in my behaviors.

But, here is a hidden presupposition in the belief system, disguised as a caring companion. While it is truly a companion, its care is only for its own voice being heard, as it is the unseen, but foundational belief, that my feelings or emotions must be given a high regard in decision making. God gave us emotions, and as such, emotions are an important part of the human psychological makeup. But the emotions were in no way designed to lead or make decisions. The main purpose for emotions is to display my belief system, not to guide it. Loss of a loved one brings expressions of grief because I have truly lost something important in my life. The sight of a beloved friend may bring to my face a warm smile, or something which I believe to be unjust may produce anger. But what I believe brings that emotion. The emotion itself is not the belief system.

But if our belief system has as one of its beliefs, that emotions and feelings are to be a part of or even lead in life decisions, emotions then take over my decision making. And a person trying to fix their damaged emotions through man-centered counseling focused on avoiding suffering and pain at all cost, will make decisions which will further damage his emotions and lead him further away from true freedom and deeper into the bondage and tyranny of Egocentricity.

Years ago I was in a meeting of elders of a church when the subject of emotions was brought up. One very wise elder said, "Emotions tell you everything." Another very wise elder stated, "Emotions tell you nothing." Both were correct. The first elder was the congregation's counselor and he was speaking of the benefit of seeing a person's belief system through his emotions. The latter elder, a very practical administrator with a doctoral degree in chemistry, was speaking of the place that emotions have in giving us direction or the making of decisions. The fact is that emotions and feelings have their place, but that place is not to lead in decisions.

Unfortunately, many, if not most, individuals are lead by their emotions. Some of the most critical decisions in our lives are overly influenced by emotional leading. Voting, marriage, promiscuity, diet, and drug and alcohol use are all influenced heavily by emotions. The outcry of plays, movies, and books is "follow your heart." Phrases such as "if it feels good do it" or "It can't be wrong if it feels so right" help to add to the confusion. Psychological philosophy is in a constant search for justification of one's aberrant behaviors and for someone on whom to blame those behaviors and relieve emotional pain. We allow artists, musicians, film directors, and news media using emotionally driven phrases and images to manipulate us into decisions and opinions which have nothing to do with righteousness or truth. Words and actions, bright with symbolism, outshine words and actions of true substance. And mankind continues the downward evolution into anarchy, created in the primordial soup of self-serving emotionalism.

At times we all may need counsel or encouragement. But what is that counsel? Is it man centered? Is it focused on curing the emotional pain that someone may be going through? Is its goal freedom from pain for the person or is the goal first the increase of His government in the individual's life, thereby bringing true and lasting freedom? Worse yet, (and I am afraid we have all seen it but hoped it was not true) is the goal the ego of the counselor in helping others or having an entourage of grateful hangers-on. I was in a recent meeting where a counselor was one of the main speakers. It was sickening, as I lost count of the times that he stated how *he* brought someone to freedom. And it is here we return to the scripture quoted at the beginning of this chapter. The Wonderful Counselor's counsel is: "So Jesus was saying to those Jews who had believed Him, 'If you continue in My word, then you are truly disciples of Mine; and you will know the truth, and the truth will make you free."

True freedom, lasting freedom comes, not from man's counseling, not from blame, not from reliance on counselors or psychological fads and theories, but from continuing, abiding in the Word of God. That abiding makes me know truth. It makes me discern error in the midst of emotional turmoil, because the Word of God changes the belief system that has caused the emotional turmoil. Those who offer counsel to others would do well to seriously ask whether the focus of their counsel is on the correct goal—is the focus on man's emotional comfort or the increase of the government of Christ in the individual. A relationship with Christ, not relationship with a counselor, therapist, or any other person will bring emotional stability and freedom into a life. The direction of our counsel must change from various techniques for coping to the one question which must be asked of all, "Are you continuing in God's Word?" The job of a true counselor, one who knows his position is merely representing the Wonderful Counselor, is to work oneself out of a job as quickly as possible, and give that job to its rightful owner, the Prince of Peace and Lord of lords, Jesus Messiah.

Chapter 9
For Mine is the Kingdom, and the Power, and the Glory

Wedding days bring visions of flowers, romance, joy, and hopes. But weddings have a way of turning into marriages. This is certainly not an attack on the institution of marriage, but when a marriage becomes an institution, the flowers, romance, joy, trust, and hope die. Emotional distance, with decreased trust and decreased communication become the norm. It is a centuries old fashion to blame the institution of marriage itself for the problem, but as is so often the case with man as judge, the judge is the guilty party. It is not the rule of marriage that is the problem, but it is rather ruling the marriage by the individual parties. Self-centeredness and lust for power are the unseen giants which destroy relationship. Self-centeredness and lust for power are the unseen giants which negate the second greatest commandment—"love thy neighbor as thyself." And lust for power and self-centeredness permeate all of mankind, for man's fallen nature comes from a fallen god—not Creator God, but creature god—Satan. And the goal of creature god and his giants is to destroy relationship, not just with man to man, but with God to man and to negate the greatest commandment, "You shall love the Lord your God with all your heart, and with all your soul, and with all your mind."

How can I love God with all my heart, soul, and mind when my mind is set on me and my desires? Jesus defined adultery, not just as a physical act, but by a heart meditating on another person for personal, selfish use. It is no different with my relationship with God. When the meditation of my heart is on me, and my love for me, and my lust for me, another god is before me, and I have created for myself an idol.

⮞ It has become fashionable to state, "My God is a God of love." Interpreted, this means, "The god I have created does not judge my selfishness and ignores any wrong doing on my part." But mankind does not have the right or ability to state, "Let us make God in our image." A god made by man does not raise man up, but pulls him down—whether the god be stone, wood, or flesh or an imagined friend. The sentiment of a "God of love" is often used in response to a mention of God's Law. The belief has become that Jesus' purpose is not to save me from my sin, but save me from the Law. Yet, this same Jesus, when speaking of love stated in John 15: 9-10, "Just as the Father has loved Me, I have also loved you; abide in My love. If you keep My commandments, you will abide in My love; just as I have kept My Father's commandments and abide in His love." Paul stated in Romans 13:10 that love is the fulfillment of the law, because love does no wrong to a neighbor. If my heart is filled with me, my behaviors will be about me, and *must result* in wrong to my neighbor. When I keep God's commandments, I abide in His love—not when I think He loves me or I "feel" love toward another person. Biblically defined love involves God's Law and commandments—they cannot be separated. Man cannot love apart from God, because God is love. Man cannot love apart from God's Law, because man is man—and will act accordingly. If man is a law unto himself, tyranny will result—not just political tyranny, but personal tyranny. When I am king, all will suffer under my kingship. When I as an individual make the laws that I and others are to live by, those laws will benefit me. The resulting strife is what most of us know simply as life— and it not "abundant". "Mine is the kingdom" will be the mind set and behaviors I have when I do not keep God's commandments. My law is not love. But the laws of God are. Meditation is simply applying the law of the king to my heart. It is listening to the commands of the king. It is the action I take to give God the rightful place of King in the Kingdom of God.

Only the Power of the King's commandments with His Life in me agreeing with those commandments can rule my rebellious soul. This is why Jesus' promise of the Holy Spirit was linked to keeping His commandments. In John 14:15-17 we read, "If you love Me, you will keep My commandments. And I will ask the Father, and He will give you another Helper, that He may be with you forever; that is the Spirit of truth, whom the world cannot receive, because it does not see Him or know Him, but you know Him because He abides with you and will be in you." Notice the main points, all connected—loving Jesus, keeping His commandments, and the promise of the Holy Spirit. My double-minded soul, listening to self, will disagree with God and fight against the Holy Spirit within me. Which is why the Bible (directed and inspired by the Holy Spirit) continually focuses on the importance of The Word. Phrases such as "washed by the water of the Word," "in the beginning was the Word," "the Word was God", "long for the true milk of the Word…to grow thereby," "the Word of the Lord came…," "the word of His power," "Your Word is truth," "preach the Word," "the Word of God is living," "the word implanted which is able to save your souls" abound in Scripture. And the Word of God is not just ordinary words. It possesses a power all its own. Hebrews 4:12 states, "For the word of God is living and active and sharper than any two-edged sword, and piercing as far as the division of soul and spirit, of both joints and marrow, and able to judge the thoughts and intentions of the heart." God's Word has a power to affect the existence, soul and spirit of mankind, not as normal, spoken words—but with a miraculous, non-naturalistic power which is not quantifiable on a cause-effect basis. It is living. It is active. It is God.

The exhortation to have my life be a life of The Word comes with a very serious problem—God's Word and ways are foreign to my life. My natural life—my flesh—is in rebellion toward God. I think humanly and I react humanly. Humanly is not Godly.

To agree with God my very nature must be changed. My soul does not naturally agree with God. And it is powerless to change—and really does not want to change. My nature must have a new nature. With this thought the "New Birth" makes sense. A new life must replace my natural life. But it must be a life that agrees with God. And the only life which will do that is God's life itself. So, God gives me a new spirit—His Spirit. God's Spirit within me agrees with God's Word. His life in me creates a new birth. Scripture literally says I am a "new creation." This new creation is a unique individual. It is a mixture of God and man. I still look like me and my person-ness (personality) is still me. But its rebellious nature is changed. I am now not the human creature I was. I am now "in Christ" and Christ is "in me." I am no longer a "natural" man; I have become a "super-natural" man; no longer *Homo sapiens* but *Theohomo*. And as a super-natural man I can now agree with God; the very life of God living in me agrees with God for me!! I am granted "righteousness"; I have become "right with God." And, as I now have a nature that agrees with God, I can agree with His Word.

True fellowship with God is agreement with His Word. Amos 3:3 states that we do not have fellowship with those with whom we disagree.

I John 2:3 states that coming to know God is keeping (Greek *tereo*) His commandments. Again, we do not have fellowship with those with whom we disagree. This has everything to do with the way to true Christian fellowship. True Christian fellowship is not agreeing with one another—it is each Christian agreeing with God's Word. Our theologies are often human attempts to coerce God into agreement with man's ideas of God. Our denominations are human efforts to coerce other men into agreement with man's ideas of God. And our feeble, faithless, and loveless attempts to cross denominational or religious lines are usually nothing more than human flailing meant to correct and cover divisions which our lust for power and control has created.

And that lust for power and control is the fertile ground for the fruit of organized religion—the common ground between Catholic, Protestant, non-denominational denominations, Muslims, or cults. Fruit in Christendom is most commonly defined with such phrases as, "Our numbers are growing," "We've had hundreds say the sinner's prayer," "We need a new (sanctuary, education building, gymnasium)," or "Take a look at all our programs."

But fruit is governed by laws, laws that God put into effect as early as creation. Fruit always comes from planting seed. And the seed always produces like kind. God put forth these laws when He created the earth. Genesis 1:24-25 states, "Then God said, "Let the earth bring forth living creatures after their kind: cattle and creeping things and beasts of the earth after their kind"; and it was so. God made the beasts of the earth after their kind, and the cattle after their kind, and everything that creeps on the ground after its kind; and God saw that it was good." All that God created were to reproduce "after their kind." Jesus stated in Matthew 7 that grapes are not gathered from thorn bushes or figs gathered from thistles. Paul tells us in Galatians 6 that a man reaps what he sows. God created the laws of genetics. They cannot be changed. Scientists manipulate genetic material and genetic traits, but they must follow the laws of genetics which God commanded. A seed always produces after its kind.

Jesus said, "I am the vine, you are the branches." My life is to bear the "fruit of the vine." The meditation of my heart produces fruit. And it always produces in like kind. One may think this sounds like "if you just wish hard enough your dreams come true," but there are serious implications in the planting of wrong seeds. Meditations produce fruit in like kind because they become part of a belief system which powers behavior. Meditation is not fantasy becoming reality; my dreams coming true.

Let me give you an example. I have found that most men who are having problems with sexual lust have a deeper problem with loneliness. The imaginations and desire for acceptance turn into imaginations and addictions to sexual lust. No five-year-old boy answers, when asked what he wants to be when he grows up, "A serial rapist and killer." But later, that five year old, hurting heart with its fifty-year-old body will do almost anything to alleviate that pain. And it began with dreams, imaginations, and meditations. It continues and grows with pornography and prostitution. And it eternally lives with the spiral of spousal and child abuse, manipulation, addictions, adultery, and the hollow scream of pain, as endless as the eternal death in which it lives, is then visited on the next generation of victims and begins the hunt anew for its own victims. Dreams of fulfilling relationships come true in the form of insatiable selfishness.

A woman may do the same thing by dreaming about being the object of attention of others and becomes that by dressing in a provocative and lewd fashion. But, as many have found out, once the attention has worn off, she will no longer be an object of attention, but merely an object. Simply dreaming about being a great sports figure or musician without the reality of hard work will only plant the fruit of disappointment, bitterness, and decreased motivation. Meditation on money and power is the seed which produces the fruit of a sense of entitlement, discontent, and rebellion. The seeds of selfish, self-gratifying meditations produce fruit precisely after their kind—a self-centered, self-deifying personality; a god who endangers self and all others; a god in need of a god; a god in need of a savior. Imaginations do not become reality; small imaginations become greater imaginations.

And here we must add that there is also a self-centered, self-deifying institution—the organized church with its dreams, imaginations, and meditations has dressed itself in a provocative and lewd fashion with worldly counsel, teaching, programs, and music. Meditation on money and power has produced a sense of entitlement, discontent, and rebellion against God's Word. The seeds of man-centered, numbers-centered, and church-growth-centered programs, no matter how we whitewash them with the "name of Jesus," produce a fruit which is anti-Christ and glorifying to the numbers of man.

God has spoken through His Son. He has very clearly defined how His disciples are to produce His fruit. He has very clearly defined how His disciples are to give glory to the Father in their production of that fruit. Jesus states in

John 15:7-8, "If you abide in Me, and My words abide in you, ask whatever you wish, and it will be done for you. By this is My Father glorified, that you bear much fruit, and so prove to be My disciples." Jesus gives us a pattern here to production of fruit His way.

"If you abide in Me" is a call to relationship. There is not one speck of religion in this statement. Religion lives in a church building. Relationship lives in one's self. The Temple of God is **not** an organization or an institution—it is the individual where the Holy Spirit dwells (I Corinthians 3:16). The word "abide" in the vernacular would be "live." We are to "live" in Christ, while on our jobs, at home, waking, sleeping, breathing. I am afraid we have missed the point of it all. It is not buildings, programs, or organizations, and certainly not the "glorious Church." Paul tells us in 2 Corinthians 6:16, "Or what agreement has the temple of God with idols? For we are the temple of the living God; just as God said, "I will dwell in them and walk among them; and I will be their God, and they shall be My people." Do not think that this is the only statement to this effect. This idea permeates Scripture. From the creation and early walks in the Garden of Eden to Emmanuel (God with us) to the outcry in Revelation of the Spirit and the Bride who say "Come," the goal of oneness with man—of man living in God and God in man has remained the same. And through this relationship God has said He will produce His fruit.

The next requirement Jesus mentions which must be present to produce fruit which is glorifying to the Father is "...My words abide in you." We have just spoken of the word abide as meaning "to live." As we are to live in Messiah, so also is His Word to live in us. Again, to "live in" is not a flippant, casual walk through an area so familiar to our knowledge that there is no knowledge. This is not a casual reading of the Word. This is not morning devotionals. This is not reading and forgetting. This is meditation, meditation to the point that the Word of God fuses with one's life. His thoughts become my thoughts, and His ways become my ways. It is deep relationship with the Word—written and incarnate. It is a deliberate, planned change of one's belief system. It is the subject of this book.

Perhaps one of the best ways to think of this is to use Jesus' analogy of a field in Mark 4:18-19: "And others are the ones on whom seed was sown among thorns; these are the ones who have heard the word, and the worries of the world, and the deceitfulness of riches, and the desires for other things enter in and choke the word, and it becomes unfruitful." You see, the Word is heard, but does not live. It has competition—the thorns from seeds of meditation on the philosophies and beliefs of the world system which say things, power, money, relationships, and fame will bring me peace, happiness, and worth. Jesus speaks of this competition in Matthew 18:8-9 when He tells us it is better to enter life crippled, lame, or blind than to have a complete body and be cast into eternal fire. The "life" here should not be taken as "eternity." It is life **now**, certainly eternal, but it started when one enters the life of the King and Kingdom that is eternal. But, we will not enter into life as it is to be lived if we do not remove the competition. Another important place where we see this principle established is in the cleansing of the temple. We see Jesus enter the temple, look around, calmly sit down and braid a whip, and then, very purposely—he removed the competition. Jesus' words abiding in me bring fruit; it is not the media's words, worldly philosophy's words, or even reading about Jesus' words that bring fruit as Jesus describes. Competing thoughts and beliefs choke the Word and make it unfruitful.

So, Jesus tells us that the closest of relationships with Him and with His Words that will bring fruit as He describes and desires. But there is one more piece to this natural progression that we have not discussed, and sadly, not just in the current treatise, but it is ignored by almost all of us in the church—organized or real, through all of history. Jesus' next statement in John 15:7 is "ask whatever you wish and it will be done for you."

"**Ask** whatever you wish, and it will be done **for** you."

"Asking" is prayer. And prayer is not a religious activity. Prayer is conversation with God; not a monologue, and not done only in church or at the bedside. It is without ceasing. This always sounded so impossible. But, this was again because of faulty, religious definitions that I had. Conversation is not simply verbal communication, and, as already stated, is not a monologue, and thus requires also listening. We do this very type of communication with other people all day long. We speak, listen, show facial and body language which indicates our thoughts on the subject, and then we may behave in accordance with the impact of that communication. ➤ All this is conversation without ceasing. And conversation between man and God without ceasing is prayer. Perhaps this can be pictured by an elderly couple that is still deeply in love after their many years together and very comfortable with themselves as individuals and have that depth of communication that does not require constant words but can be conveyed by the movement of a hand, a micro movement of the face unperceivable by all save the partner, a sigh in the night.

"**Ask** whatever you wish, and it will be done **for** you."

The independent, arrogant mind of man—even those who are Christian—interprets Jesus' statement as, "I am going this way or I am doing this. You, God, are to come along and help." But Jesus did not say that He would help. He said "ask and it will be done for you." Church programs, denominations, the latest church growth fad, Paul's great learning and accomplishments, your and my great learning and accomplishments are all dung in comparison to having and knowing Christ. And none of these are the way to bear fruit as Jesus said: "Asking" and allowing God to do it "for" us is the way in which we bear much fruit and Father is glorified. All our fleshly efforts do bear fruit, but not to the glory of Father, but rather to the glory of mankind, church-kind, religious-kind—the Tower of Babel rising to make a name above the Name above all names. In the famous verse of Revelation 13:18 regarding the beast we see stated, "the number is that of a man and his number is six hundred and sixty-six." The Greek in this sentence reveals a subtlety. There is no definite article "a" in the Greek. In other words, the phrase "a man" is not there. There are two most commonly used words for man. One is *andros*, which is usually used for an individual man or husband, i.e., "a man." This is not the word used in this sentence. The word used is *anthropos*, whose primary meaning is mankind as a whole, universally mankind or man as a species. So perhaps a better understanding of the sentence is not in terms of a specific man (which may be true), but of mankind as a whole, in his pride opposed to Christ's kingship in his life. We keep looking for a world leader to rise up and be the anti-Christ, when it is mankind as a whole who, in his pride, in his self-sufficiency, and in his pompous assumption of the role of building the church is "Anti Christ." It is mankind looking at the I Am and stating "Not You. I am". Anti Christ is me.

And there is no need to fear the phrase "whatever you wish," for anyone who lives in Messiah and in whom

Messiah's words live, will have his or her wishes changed from those of this world to the wishes of God. Psalm 37:4 states to delight yourself in the Lord and he will give you the desires of your heart." If you are delighting yourself in the Lord, the desires of your heart will not be for worldly things, for He will give your heart new desires; desires of and from the heart which is all love. Asking whatever you wish will not be the wishes of a worldly, double-minded, anti-Christ heart—it will be from a heart filled with the wishes of the true Christ.

For according to the verses upon which we have been focused, "If you abide in Me, and My words abide in you, ask whatever you wish, and it will be done for you. By this is My Father is glorified, that you bear much fruit, and so prove to be My disciples". The glorification of Father and the production of much fruit is **answered prayer**.

Chapter 10
Memorize, Meditate, and Marriage

To repeat the last chapter, wedding days bring visions of flowers, romance, joy, and hopes. But weddings have a way of turning into marriages. This is certainly not an attack on the institution of marriage, but when a marriage becomes an institution the flowers, romance, joy, and hope die. One of the problems, as shown earlier, is our overemphasis on feelings. Emotions are almost always involved in a decision to marry. But emotions cool. And a good thing they do. If the emotional feelings of that first felt romantic love permeated us for 24 hours a day, all the days of our lives, little would be accomplished in any life. Unfortunately, our reliance on emotions to dictate "love" or actions from that love is the very thing which eventually brings about the death of so many marriages. Because those exciting emotions are based on the false hopes that the person married will meet my deepest emotional needs and that their only thought will be to satisfy my personal wants. That may work if only one person is in the marriage, but most marriages consist of two people. And this, again, is where Self gets in the way—or more precisely, both Selves. Both partners believe they are in charge and the marriage is for their pleasure and convenience. Egos reign. Self is king.

It always bears repeating: the kingdom of God is God's life ruling in the life of the individual. We will only be "as gods" as God is in us. Satan stated to Eve that we would be like God when we knew good and evil; God says you will be like God when we know Him—the one Good— intimately; when God, through faith and relationship actually lives in you; when man and God become one. This is not blasphemy; this is the good news. It has already happened when Christ was on this earth in a body; it now happens in we who are the body of Christ. This is the true atonement—the true "At one-ment." The true church is the bride of Christ; at one with Him. Ephesians 5:32 tells us "this mystery is great; but I am speaking with reference to Christ and the church." What mystery? It is that the two become one flesh. This is Christ and the church; this is man and wife.

But something has obviously gone wrong. Not only do we see little of the oneness between man and God, but a true oneness between man and wife has always been rare. Adultery is not a modern disease. The problem remains; and remains as obvious as it has for all the ages—the two have not become one, because the two are determined to be The One Alone; to be god without being one with God. Man's creation of oneness is not one new creature being formed from two, but one creature, alone in the darkness of a tightly shut room, announcing to all (no one is there), "I Am Oneness." Man without God will always remain—man; man alone. What is the answer to man's inability to become one with even his or her marriage partner—the closest of human covenants?

— We have already mentioned the mystery in Ephesians 5 and it is here where we find the answer to our question. Verse 22 states, "Wives be subject to your own husbands, as to the Lord." Few Biblical concepts have been more poorly applied than this one. Husbands shout "Amen", and wives whisper "How?" Left out, of course, is the preceding verse which says, "be subject to one another in the fear of Christ." (Wives and husbands both sit in stunned, unbelieving silence.) What does the tyrannical or even patriarchal husband do with such a statement? I have never heard that verse preached on or emphasized in regards to marriage structure. We have understood "headship" through—again—the self-focused belief system of me. Headship, Biblical headship, has nothing to do with anyone being the boss or with the husband as king and master. True Biblical headship is about the sacrifice of one's life and protection of those under that headship. This is the pattern of Christ. This is the greater love.

But before we go further, we must notice what Paul is doing in this passage—he is creating an analogy comparing Christ and the church to husband and wife. To fully understand the message here we must follow the analogy through the entire passage. Verse 23 states, "For the husband is the head of the wife, as Christ also is the head of the church, He Himself being the Savior of the body." And here we begin to see the true nature of the passage— Savior. Using the analogy we can easily say that Christ, as the head of the church is the savior of the church, and the husband, as the head of the wife is the savior of the wife. Certainly, human husbands are not saviors as Christ is the eternal or the universal sense. The problem with our understanding is again, the religious way in which we think. The word in the Greek for savior is defined by Dr. Spiros Zodhiates as "A savior, deliverer, preserver, one who saves from danger or destruction and brings into a state of prosperity and happiness." Jesus is all of these things; so also, is the husband to be to his wife. The Biblical concept of headship (husbandship) is not that of rule, but that of responsibility; not boss, but benefactor; not slave owner, but servant.

Paul then speaks about the wife as she compares to the church: "But as the church is subject to Christ, so also the wives ought to be to their husbands in everything." But how, in a loving relationship, can the wife be subject to their husbands in everything? Paul tells us as "the church is subject to Christ." The organized church knows little or nothing of this concept. Organized religion exists for itself and requires subservience, not of love but of lust. Christ is not the head of organized religion, be it the "church", temple, mosque, or synagogue. The pastor, pope, bishop, rabbi, priest, monk, cleric is the head of whatever they have named the monster they rule. The only way that the church, voluntarily loving God, can be subject to Christ is by agreeing with Christ—not a doctrinal dung heap where the worm dieth not. The belief system of the body, the church, must be the same as the belief system of Christ, the head. Christ's belief system is of the Word. For the church to have the belief system of Christ, it must "receive the Word implanted, which is able to save your soul." My belief system becomes the belief system which is Christ's belief system; I agree with the written Word, as the Incarnate Word's power lives within me. My belief system, as it agrees with God's belief system, lets me trust God. Trust is not an emotion anymore than love is an emotion. Trust is the response of my will to the belief system established in my heart.

How does this relate to a wife being subject to her husband? For most, the first thought is to state that this means the wife simply agrees with the husband on all things. This is so far from the heart of God that its rejection should have been immediate; but, as we have noted, man is for man, self for self. The true answer is given in the analogy. Verse 22 states wives are to be subject to their husbands "as to the Lord." To be subject to someone voluntarily requires the person who is being subject to trust the one in charge. We have demanded that wives do something which they cannot do—fully trust another human. They not only cannot do so, no where does Scripture tell her to do so. The subjection comes in the wife's trusting the Lord—it comes in her relationship with God; from her meditation on Scripture. It is as we have just mentioned. The church is not subject to the Lord when it "chooses" to be so. The church is subject to the Lord when it agrees with God's word. The wife is not subject to the husband when she agrees with the husband's words or ways, but when she agrees with the Lord's words and ways. It is not trusting in the husband—it is trusting in God. The church should not trust in itself, its pastors, it popes, its doctrines—it will only be subject to God when it agrees with God—when it agrees with God's Word. Man and wife walk as a single unit when they are agreed; not agreed in human opinion, but both individually agreeing with God's Word. That agreement of two comes from meditation of one; and the two become one.

In I Peter 3, the subject again is the wife's submissiveness to her husband in the Lord. In verse 4 we are told, "but let it be the hidden person of the heart, with the imperishable quality of a gentle and quiet spirit, which is precious in the sight of God." It sounds simple enough, but how does one have "a gentle and quiet spirit?" We are told to "let it be the hidden person of the heart." And there is the clue we need. "Thy word have I hid in my heart." "My son let your heart keep my commandments." The hidden person of the heart gains the quality of a gentle and quiet spirit through meditation on God's word; through the relationship of sitting at the feet of Jesus and allowing his life to live in me. And oddly, that is the duty the wife has to her husband on earth, and her heavenly husband as a member of the church—"keep His commandments." When one keeps the commandments of God through meditation, trust is gained. A wife will always have difficulty fully "trusting" her husband.

He is human, fallible, and finite. But she is commanded to trust Father. And Biblical submission to a husband is not submission to the husband—it is submission through meditation and relationship to God.

But we must return to the analogy. The passage speaks much more to the husband than to the wife. Paul continues, "Husbands, love your wives, just as Christ also loved the church and gave Himself up for her, so that He might sanctify her, having cleansed her by the washing of water with the word, that He might present to Himself the church in all her glory, having no spot or wrinkle or any such thing; but that she would be holy and blameless."

Husbands are to love their wives just as Christ loved the church. How did Christ love the church? He laid down his life for her. He gave himself up for her. Jesus stated "Greater love has no one than this that one lay down his life for his friends." Laying down one's life is the greatest love. The Greek word for life is quite different than we normally think. Our picture is one of a physical martyr, dying a biological death for one's beliefs. But the word here is not the word for biological life; it is the word for "soul." The greater love is laying down one's soul. The Greek word for "soul" is *psyche*. It is defined as, and best understood Biblically, as the seat of the mind, emotions, and will. This is what man and animals have in common. Animals and man think and learn (the mind); they have fear and happiness (emotions); and they purpose and perform behaviors (the will). Applying this to Jesus' statement of greater love gives us the understanding "Greater love has no one than this that one lay down his mind (what I think), his emotions (what I feel), his will (what I want) for his friends." Laying down one's life is not laying down one's death; it is a living death; a death to self; a death to living life for self. Laying down my life is putting aside what I want and giving the best for the person loved. (As an aside for singles: Christ laid his life down for the church _before_ there was a church. Success in marriage begins before marriage.)

If we truly understand this concept, the idea of physical martyrdom would be welcomed compared to the thought of this living death. Jesus has called us to nothing less than what He walked. He only did, thought, and spoke as the Father willed; for the joy which was before Him (you) He endured the cross. Paul tells us. "that our old self was crucified with Him, in order that our body of sin might be done away with, so that we would no longer be slaves to sin." The concern here is not some life in the ethereal future, but my life now, on this earth, in this body. "It is no longer I who live, but Christ lives in me." This is not a pithy, cute cliché or slogan to hang on our walls and lips like some dead trophy. Christ is the spiritual, incarnate Word; in His usual (at least to us) somewhat abstract form unseen and not perceived physically. It is the written Word of God placed in me which is the concrete form of the Word that connects me to the life (the Spirit and Soul) of Christ Jesus; and with that connection—that new belief system with self as dead, and the Love of God in Christ alive to others. The husband's duty, in our analogy is not to lay down his biological life (which may happen), but to lay down his living, his way of life, his wants and needs for the sake of his wife. This can only be done when the belief system of the husband is the belief system of the Christ; one the Savior of the world, the other the savior of the wife.

And this is exactly how Jesus laid down His life for the church. Sanctification simply means being set apart. Being "set apart" does not happen magically; it again is the function of one's belief system. it is the belief system of a soldier that sets him apart to fight. It is the belief system of the individual in various religions and denominations that separates them from others. It is the belief system of the true disciple of Christ that sets him apart from the world. John 17:19 states, "For their sakes I sanctify Myself, that they themselves also may be sanctified in truth." Jesus sanctified Himself that we might be sanctified. The mystery of being one with Jesus is that who He is I am; where He is I am; what He has done I have done; when I am somewhere He has already been and is now; when He sanctified Himself, I became sanctified. But we must note He said, "sanctified in truth." How is one sanctified in truth? Jesus explains this two verses before in John 17:17 "Sanctify them in the truth; Your word is truth." It is the Word that sanctifies. And in this case, the Word and the mysterious oneness between Christ and His church sanctify both. And in the case of the husband and wife, the Word and the mysterious oneness between husband and wife sanctify both.

Why would these "saviors" desire the church and the wife to be "saved" and for what purpose? The very next verse of our text in Ephesians 5 tells us: "so that He might sanctify her, having cleansed her by the washing of water with the word, that He might present to Himself the church in all her glory, having no spot or wrinkle or any such thing; but that she would be holy and blameless." The purpose of Christ and the husband laying down their lives (desires, wishes, thoughts) is that the wife (or church) be sanctified by washing of the water of the word that the wife (or church) may be presented to himself (either the husband or Christ). Christ is presenting the church—the perfect, beautiful church to Himself; the husband is presenting his beautiful, perfect wife to himself. It almost sounds selfish. I have had husbands tell me they were concerned that their desire to have a good relationship with their wife was not a good reason to engraft God's Word; that they did not have the right attitude in seeking God in this way; that meditating on God's Word to win their wife was hypocritical. But since when did I ever come to Christ with a perfect attitude of and from myself? Many come to Christ to escape hell; we love Him because He first loved us; we want to sacrifice, believing that there is reward to be gained. Search your heart—you will never come to Christ of a pure, altruistically motivated heart—unless it is given by Him to you. We come to the Father through Christ, not because we want to, but because we perceive that it is best for us. (And even that perception is given by Him.) According to this verse, Christ wants the church for Himself. Evidently that is "okay." As such, it must also be "okay" (and certainly preferred by the wife) for the husband to want the wife. So, Christ desires the church to be "saved" (holy and blameless) so that He may present her to Himself. He does so by "washing her with the water of the Word."

This washing by the Word is **not** done by the husband studying the Word and preaching or teaching his wife. Again, it is through the mysterious oneness of the two becoming one. When the husband receives the Word through meditation, his wife mysteriously receives the benefit of that Word in her; she is washed by the water of the Word.

The one section of Scripture that is probably the most depressing to the majority of believing wives is Proverbs 31. No matter how one may twist it or present it or sugar coat it or try to kill it, it still says the same thing to the woman: "This is an impossible standard for a wife." And so, the wife sees the goal and finds the goal is not reachable, and she gives up in despair. But there is a good reason the wife finds this

Scripture difficult; it was not written to her. It was written to the husband. Just the first few verses tell us that:

→ 10 An excellent wife, who can find?
  (She is not trying to find an
  excellent wife.)
For her worth is far above jewels.
  (Her worth is not to her self but to her
  husband.)
11 The heart of her husband trusts in her,
  (It is the heart of her <u>husband</u> that trusts.)
And he will have no lack of gain.
  (<u>He</u> has no lack of gain.)
12 She does him good and not evil
  (She does <u>him</u> good.)
All the days of her life

You see the point—Proverbs 31 is written to the man, not the woman. And, as such, it is the man's responsibility to bring the woman to the picture of a "Proverbs 31 wife"; not through overbearing demand, but through his laying down his soul for her, by sanctifying her in that truth through his meditation on that Scripture—not her meditations or her actions. Christ "kept" Father's commandments and words, resulting in His sanctification, and then the sanctification of the church; the husband "keeps" God's words (and the Incarnate Word) resulting in his sanctification and then the sanctification of the wife. I Corinthians 13 states that love "hopes all things" and that "love never fails." The hope is not in a human, whether man or woman; but rather the hope is in what God's Word says the person is. It is God's Word that sanctifies, saves the soul, washes the church and the wife, and by which we grow.

Unfortunately, this also works on wrong meditations. If the husband meditates on evil, the wife receives of that meditation also. But the fruit of such meditations is not as one may wish. All husbands (and wives) have evil thoughts which cross their minds. This is temptation. (I must add here that temptation is normal; but frequent, strong temptation is not normal to the Believer, and its strength and frequency is increased by musing, daydreaming, meditating on the temptation. Jesus said, "who looks at a woman **with lust** for her has committed adultery with her **in his heart**." "Seeing" a woman is not lust; looking with lust is meditation in the heart and is equivalent to the act of adultery. The more one meditates with lust, the more one will be tempted to meditate to lust.)

Someone may be tempted to think, "My dreams will come true. If I think about my lusts a lot, so will my wife and she will want to frequently participate in whatever perversity I have imagined." But the same seed planted in various types of soil does not produce the same fruit in every soil. Shallow, alkaline soil will not produce the same fruit from an oak's acorn brought from an acidic swamp; genetically it will be the same, functionally and in appearance it will be quite different. A woman's soul is different than a man's soul; the fruit from such meditation by the man produces **in kind**, not exactly. A husband meditating on sexual lust will not produce in his wife a desire for sexual lust; he will produce fear in her. Remember, the husband and wife are one. And also remember that a man meditating with lust in his heart is performing the equivalent of adultery. The wife (at one with her husband) senses her displacement and begins to experience unnatural and frequent fear. You see, the seed planted has not produced what the husband wants; it has produced what he does not want; but it has produced in kind.

He fears losing out on his lust; his wife fears losing her place as a wife. His lust is about his selfish wants; his wife responds with her own selfish wants. And do not think that the husband is the only guilty party here. A wife meditating on romance novels or serial melodramas will, by her dreaming, plant more lust and egotism within the husband. Her dream will come true; but not the dream of a romantic prince sweeping her off her feet to live happily ever after, but rather of a self-centered king of his castle and the slavery which ensues from egotistical tyranny.

The wife is not a weak participant in this area. Scripture states that the husband is to live with his wife in an understanding way, as with a weaker vessel—it never says she is a weaker vessel. The best way to see this is by asking a question: "Which holds more liquid: a 10 ounce metal cup or a 10 ounce paper cup?" The obvious answer is that both hold the same. But there is a difference. The metal cup is hard and often unbending, easily representing the "stronger" male. The paper cup is more sensitive and responsive to its environment, hence the wife. But both hold the same amount of the Holy Spirit. One is not weaker than the other, but is more sensitive; not worth less, but designed for a different function. And it is of vital importance that especially the husband, be the leader in the sanctification by the Word. Jesus was very clear that it is when the strong man is bound that his house if plundered. Our homes are being plundered of peace, family members, joy, and the blessings of the Kingdom of God because the strong man is bound—bound by selfishness and ungodly meditations, resulting not in sanctification, being set aside for Christ, but instead with pollution and weakness because of being bound to Satan and the worldly system of selfishness.

Matthew 16:18 tells up very clearly, it is Christ's responsibility to build the church. Man has wrongly taken that responsibility, with rather ridiculous results. But man does have specific responsibilities; those related to the death of his own wishes and resurrected life to others. That life comes from The Life, Jesus Christ, flowing through the life of man. But the death to self only comes when the belief system of man is the belief system of God; and that only comes through meditation on His Word. The Bible calls that new belief system "sanctification"; a setting aside for a specific purpose. This holds particularly true in marriage, where two have individuals have become one individual.

This chapter would not be written at all if the healing of my own marriage had not happened due directly to meditation. The freedom and joy my wife and I discovered, as we found one another through God and His Word was the beginning of a life of joy and adventure in the Eternal which has far surpassed anything which we romantically dreamed or thought possible. And as we walked in His way we told others. And others began to experience in their marriages the same life we had found. It is not an overnight, drive-through quick emotional fix; this is a way of life; an everlasting life. We have watched through the years as many would hear the message of sanctification of self and the family via the engrafting of the Word; many were called, but only a few chose the path. Those that embarked on a life of agreement with God's Word through meditation had consistently strong and healthy marriages. Those who turned their backs for easier, quick fixes continued with much less than what God had for them in their marriages; the bride, adorned for her husband and a husband laying down his life for his wife after the fashion of Jesus for His bride.

Chapter 11
The Anger of Man Does Not Achieve the Righteousness of God

Emotions were created by God and are therefore, inherently good. They are part of the make-up of a normal human psyche. But we as humans have little understood the proper use of our emotions. Emotions have become our leaders, our beliefs, our directors with little understanding of what their original intended purpose was. Emotions and "feelings" were never meant to make decisions for direction. Emotions tell us what we believe; they are the window into the belief system of a person; windows into the mind. Emotions tell me what I like, what I dislike, what I want, what I think I want, who I think I want. They do not tell me fact.

This was discussed at length earlier and as such we will not overly dwell on it again. But there is one emotional response which is common to man and causes damage or death to millions of lives everyday—anger. It is not my intent to discuss anger and all its effects and causes, but rather to give answers to its defeat in the believer's life.

Every troubled word of this book has been, unfortunately, lived by me personally. I was a very angry man. But, God had again, quietly done the impossible in me. One day I was attending a men's conference where I was to speak on the benefits of meditation on God's Word. I had flown in late and quietly entered the auditorium just to check the tenor of the meeting. The speaker had finished his talk and quite a discussion was taking place regarding anger. Men were confessing anger, asking for prayer, and asking for answers. As I listened to this, I was suddenly struck by something which I had not realized had happened to me—I was no longer constantly angry. In fact, I could not remember the last time I had been angry. Now, unless you are an angry person and you know it, and have never been able to do anything about it that may not mean much. But to those of us who have lived a life of anger, such a revelation is a shock. I almost blurted out loud, "Lord, what has happened to me?" He kindly began to answer and when I returned to my room that night, he led me to the following verses in the first chapter of James:

> 19 This you know, my beloved brethren. But everyone must be quick to hear, slow to speak and slow to anger;
> 20 for the anger of man does not achieve the righteousness of God.
> 21 Therefore, putting aside all filthiness and all that remains of wickedness, in humility receive the word implanted, which is able to save your souls.
> 22 But prove yourselves doers of the word, and not merely hearers who delude themselves.
> 23 For if anyone is a hearer of the word and not a doer, he is like a man who looks at his natural face in a mirror;
> 24 for once he has looked at himself and gone away, he has immediately forgotten what kind of person he was.
> 25 But one who looks intently at the perfect law, the law of liberty, and abides by it, not having become a forgetful hearer but an effectual doer, this man will be blessed in what he does

Verse 19 gives us one of those statements which sound so right and practical—and of course, it is—but, when considered, is completely impossible. "OK, Christian, all you have to do is be quick to hear others, don't speak your own words too fast, and don't get angry very fast." And then we are left hanging and screaming the question, "HOW?"

But, the answer is there in verse 21: "Therefore." It is an old, but accurate statement, that when one sees a "therefore", look to see what it is there for. In this case the subject of the "therefore" is the tongue and anger. "Therefore" to be quick to hear, slow to speak, and slow to anger:

- put aside all filthiness
  - o   i.e. repent of your sins
- put aside all that remains of wickedness
  - o   i.e. seek to be holy (wholly) given to Christ
- in humility, receive the word implanted, which is able to save
  your souls
  - o   meditate on the Word.

The first two actions in this list are the norm for most true Christians. Repentance over sin and a desire to follow Christ is what we hear and are taught consistently in most churches, even those that don't really mean it. Obviously, it is the last point in this list in which we are interested and how it relates to anger.

"In humility" is the attitude in which we are to receive God's Word. You see, we usually spend most of our time "receiving" my own word or the word of others. By "receive" I don't just mean we physically hear it; we receive it; take it in; think on it; hold it; meditate on it; agree with it. It becomes part of me. "In humility" is a phrase which means I agree with God's Word and not my own. It is agreeing with God's assessment of the situation, especially the situation of me. This is actually true confession. Confession is simply verbally agreeing with God's Word's view of me. When I sin I have violated God's Law which causes separation from

Him; but His Word also says I am in Him and He is faithful to forgive. But if I do not agree with the fact that I have violated His Law, I cannot be forgiven; because I have not <u>received</u> the Word which says I have done wrong and must be forgiven. And it is only when I "humble" my belief (the belief which says, "I've done no wrong.") under the Word of God ("All have sinned", "Sin is a transgression of the Law.") that I can receive the Word that I cannot undo my sin, but can only humbly receive His forgiveness.

Humbly receiving the Word is to choose God's Words over my words. But James does not stop there. He states we are to "receive the Word <u>implanted</u>." Implanted is a different level. A seed can just be thrown on the ground or it may be implanted; buried; hidden. The Authorized Version uses the word "engrafted." It is the picture of depth and oneness. To implant is to place a seed into the depths of soil and to engraft would be to make two plants into one. Either way, the meaning is clear—this is not a casual reading of the Word, but truly receiving it as a new nature and life within me. Yes, it is yet another of the countless pictures of meditation. It is meditation which creates beliefs within me; which makes two (my mind and God's Word) become one. This is engrafting. Something of a new and different nature has permeated and infused itself with the nature that was me and has changed the basic makeup of me. I have received the Word implanted which is able to save my soul.

And it is my soul where the problem originates. The problem is not the emotion of anger. Emotions, as has been pointed out, are inherently good and are not evil. They are the windows to the mind; a snapshot of a deeper problem. And that deeper problem is in my mind's belief system. Emotions tell us what the mind believes. And this is the problem in the soul. As has been discussed earlier the soul consists of the mind, the will, and the emotions. All my emotions can be traced to the belief system in my mind. Therefore, the answer to problem emotions is not in resisting the emotions—it is to change the belief system. Changing the emotions is not possible.

An often used phrase is "I must control my emotions." But you see one cannot do so. Such control is simply controlling the outward evidence of an inward emotion. The emotion still lives. All that was controlled was the outward expression of the emotion. The will to hide the outward expression only overcame the outward expression of the inward emotion. The emotional feeling still exists; the outward expression has been stuffed down into the psyche where it festers and I am seen as "Stoic" or "Brave" or "Hard", when actually it is simply my will overcoming the expression of emotion; not overcoming the emotion itself. And those "repressed" emotions still live, and still hurt, and will be expressed in some form; and will cause damage to self and others.

How does the will overcome the expression of felt emotion? It will often be through thoughts such as, "I must remain strong and not cry" or "It would not be appropriate to laugh now" or "As a Christian I cannot be angry." And with those thoughts I "will" my felt emotion to not express itself. But it is apparent that the will is actually the expression of something other than itself. My will is expressing my beliefs from my mind. In this case, the belief in my mind that a particular emotion should not be expressed is stronger than the belief which triggered the emotion.

Which brings us again to the main point of this discussion: the source of emotions and the strength of the will—the belief system in the mind. James 4:1-2 states,

108

> ⚘"What is the source of quarrels and conflicts among you? Is not the source your pleasures that wage war in your members?
> You lust and do not have; so you commit murder. You are envious and cannot obtain; so you fight and quarrel."

The outward expression of inward desires is quarrels and conflicts. The outward expression of lust is murder. The outward expression of envy is fighting and quarreling. Beliefs beget behavior.

It is not out of control emotions that cause my problems. It is the inward belief system which drives those emotions which I have refused to control. That belief system is self-centered, telling me I deserve to have cars, money, relationships, respect, power; it tells me I am king. I, of course, never stop to realize that is what I believe, because the belief system also tells me I don't believe such things and that I am one of the kindest, most just, patient, and giving people on this earth. My belief system is constantly, quietly speaking to me that I am good, that I do things correctly, that it is others who are my problem, and, most importantly, that I do not think myself to be good, correct, or arrogant; and this is its greatest strengths—its own arrogance and self-centeredness hides its arrogance and self-centeredness. Jeremiah 17:9 states, "The heart is more deceitful than all else and is desperately sick; who can understand it?" I literally hide me from me. And my belief system hides behind the facade of emotions. Emotions may be the window to the belief system of the soul, but they are a dark window.

Oddly enough, the path of this discussion has led us to the main subject on which the Lord Jesus Christ preached; one which we almost completely ignore and which we little understand—the Kingdom of God (or the Kingdom of Heaven).   Jesus came preaching, "Repent, for the kingdom of heaven is at hand."   We have equated the Kingdom of God with the church or we have exiled the Kingdom of God from the present to the future.   Both of these lies are perfect for keeping man from the power that a working, cooperative, and loving relationship with God the Father brings. (For those who have been taught and believe that the Kingdom of God is in heaven and only in the future, an appendix of Scriptures has been included at the end of this book for you to consider.) The Kingdom of God is more readily understood if we think of it as the **Kingship of God** in the individual life—a life in which God rules--now.   This, of course, is basic Christian doctrine—not for the future but for the present. We simply do not think of His Kingdom in those terms. Mankind as a whole could only submit to the rule of God when mankind as a whole was redeemed to no longer serve his masters—Satan and self.   For that to be accomplished a representative of all mankind must live in the freedom of God perfectly, and then present that perfect life before God as an exchange (redemption) of all mankind. With that accomplished, man, the individual could **now** live under the rule of a loving God, rather than the evil of Satan and the taskmasters of self actualization and self gratification. This is what Jesus accomplished for you. You lived and died in the perfect representative for all of mankind.   But that perfect representative was perfect because He submitted fully to God's rule—God's kingdom; thus bringing the Kingdom of Heaven to Earth. Jesus said, "Seek **first** His kingdom and His righteousness" and therefore, it is vital that we understand the concept of His Kingdom.

But it is also vital that we understand the other part of His preaching: "Repent." The English definitions all involve some statement of "feeling" regret or remorse. But the Greek word found in the New Testament is quite different. It is the word transliterated *metanoeo* and comes from two words, *meta*, meaning to change, and *noeo*, perceptions or the mind. The Hebrew word for repent means much the same—**change your mind**. While emotions may result from a new understanding and grief over wrong actions, the true meaning of the word is clearly a deliberate, non-emotional call to change your mind. So we see the literal good news, "gospel" message teaching of Christ was, "Change your belief system, because the kingship of God is here."

Isn't it interesting that we hear Christian teachers stating—and we know it to be truth—that no one can obey God's law. Mankind is imperfect and his very nature is disobedience. And yet, often in the same sentence and breath we demand obedience, and claim God demands it also. We try to overcome this apparent (and real) contradiction by arguing that the Believer in Christ has been born again and now has a new nature which obeys God, while ignoring that the evidence of nature shows that to be patently false. While it is true we have been given a new nature, it is not a nature which obeys God, but a new nature which <u>can</u> obey God. From experience we see that there appears to be a life within me which continues to disagree with obedience to God; from Scripture we hear Paul speaking of this fight in Romans 7:

> 15 For what I am doing, I do not understand; for I am not practicing what I would like to do, but I am doing the very thing I hate.
> 16 But if I do the very thing I do not want to do, I agree with the Law, confessing that the Law is good.

17 So now, no longer am I the one doing it, but sin which dwells in me.

18 For I know that nothing good dwells in me, that is, in my flesh; for the willing is present in me, but the doing of the good is not.

19 For the good that I want, I do not do, but I practice the very evil that I do not want.

20 But if I am doing the very thing I do not want, I am no longer the one doing it, but sin which dwells in me.

21 I find then the principle that evil is present in me, the one who wants to do good.

22 For I joyfully concur with the law of God in the inner man,

23 but I see a different law in the members of my body, waging war against the law of my mind and making me a prisoner of the law of sin which is in my members

24 Wretched man that I am! Who will set me free from the body of this death

And this, of course, brings us back to our main subject of meditation, and another of those important secrets hidden in the Word of God. We have already seen that "keeping" God's commandments is not obeying—it is meditation upon them. But there is another word which is translated in the New Testament as "obey" or "obedience", while the literal meaning is quite different. Romans 6 states:

15 What then? Shall we sin because we are not under law but under grace? May it never be!

16 Do you not know that when you present yourselves to someone as slaves for obedience, you are slaves of the one whom you obey, either of sin resulting in death, or of obedience resulting in righteousness?

17 But thanks be to God that though you were slaves of sin, you became obedient from the heart to that form of teaching to which you were committed,

18 and having been freed from sin, you became slaves of righteousness.

19 I am speaking in human terms because of the weakness of your flesh. For just as you presented your members as slaves to impurity and to lawlessness, resulting in further lawlessness, so now present your members as slaves to righteousness, resulting in sanctification

The real purpose of Paul's argument here is not to state as some falsely do, that the Law has been done away and has no purpose in the life of the Believer. I John 3:4 states that sin is a transgression of the Law. Therefore, if the Law has been done away, as many now state, there is no sin and God has no standard with which to judge. A criminal court may throw out a sentence on someone, but it does not throw out the law.

But the truly amazing thing hidden in his argument is that the literal translation of the word "obey" or "obedience" is actually "**listen to**." So verse 16 would read: "Do you not know that when you present to someone as slaves for listening, you are slaves of the one to whom you listen, either of sin resulting in death, or of listening resulting in righteousness?" You see the difference and its agreement with the rest of Scripture. God is very certain we will not obey Him with our own strength—so He gives us His Holy Spirit to obey in us and for us. But, I still have that part of me that says "No!"; that part of me that does not agree with God—my belief system, which for years has **listened to** and believed the world and self. So, rather than demand that I obey His Law, He asks that I **listen to** His law—to meditate on His law day and night (Psalm 1).

And this brings us back to the subject of the book—meditation—and the subject of this chapter—anger. We have seen that my basic nature, my flesh, is opposed to God, until He gives me a new nature—His nature, His life, Immanuel, God with us. We have also seen that my belief system is opposed to God, until He gives me a new belief system—His Word through meditation. His nature in me now agrees with His word in me, and obedience is no longer the problem.

You see, my struggle against anger has not been the correct path to overcoming anger. The way to overcome anger is to change my belief system to God's belief system. God is not lustful, covetous, jealous, or self-centered, and when I have His belief system as my belief system, I am not lustful, covetous, jealous, or self-centered. And, as such, I am also not angry, because I no longer function in the belief system that life is about my wants and desires. Jesus said in Mark 9:35, "If anyone wants to be first, he shall be last of all and servant of all." When I desire to be last, I will not demand to be first. My wants and desires (the source of quarrels and conflicts) are no longer the lords of my behaviors, but with Jesus as Lord, and His Holy Spirit as the power in my life, and His Word as the belief system in my life, the wants and desires of God and those I love become the lords of my behaviors. Instead of anger fueled by my desires, I now have love, fueled by the desire to serve others.

Through meditation upon the Word of God, my worldly, self-centered belief system is replaced by God's spiritually, other-centered (loving) belief system and His Holy Spirit, in agreement with that new belief system now results in Godly, loving behavior. My anger has been replaced with love, as I no longer walk by the flesh, but by the power of the Spirit, with my soul agreeing with God's ways. I, through meditation and the indwelling of God's very life, have become "quick to hear, slow to speak, and slow to anger." God is love, and His life in me now lives that love free from the demands of a belief system which directs and empowers anger. I have received "implanted the Word, which is able to save my soul."

Chapter 12
The Love of Law and the Law of Love

The most amazing fact about man when he compromises is the fact that he will be amazed and surprised that he has compromised. Jeremiah 17:9 states, "The heart is more deceitful than all else and is desperately sick; who can understand it." Often ignored facts of my life in this world are my frequent compromise and my ancient, devious enemy who is Compromise. And the more interesting fact which follows these two facts is that we really believe neither fact. I believe MY beliefs are all correct, and I believe MY church/denomination/theology is correct. And I absolutely do not believe—that I am influenced in my beliefs by Satan. The "I" within me firmly believes my thoughts are my thoughts (or they are God's thoughts) and are not open to question, by others or even myself. I never stop to actually realize that the enemy of my soul was the anointed cherub, who has been successfully deceiving men and angels for thousands of years, and that he may appear as an angel (Lit. messenger) of light to me, and just might be of higher intellect than I!! And, he is very capable of using the Word of God to deceive as he attempted to do with Jesus, using the part to pervert the whole.

The saying "If you can't beat 'em, join 'em" is not Scriptural and is not from God; it is of Compromise; it is from Satan; and he is its master. When Pharaoh could not beat Moses, he feigned obeisance; when Balak could not defeat Israel, Balaam counseled to join Israel; when Satan realized that he could not stop the early church, he joined it and has not withdrawn his membership. His goal in creating creeds, denominations, dominations, popes, and protrusive pastors has been one thing—to negate the Word of God. The goal must always be: negate the Word of God. In the beginning was the Word—and Satan said, "Has God said..." In the ending the dragon continues "to make war with those who keep the commandments of God and hold to the testimony of Jesus."

And now here is the great subtlety of Satan and his abilities—he has chosen the greatest of words and the greatest of commandments to bring about the greatest of compromises. He has suggested and taught from pulpits, Protestant and Popish, that the greatest of commandments, to love, is disconnected from and has negated all other commandments; that love has done away with law. Nothing could be farther from the truth, and closer to his heart.

And his next step has been to re-define the word "love" humanistically rather than Godly, emotionally and erotically rather than rationally; to invite us, in pity, kindness, and tolerance toward our fellow creature; to set our mind on man's interests rather than God's; to settle for shack and shed rather than the True Sanctuary.

We hear it most often expressed in the phrase, "I have a God of love" coupled (lovingly) with a look of condescending superiority. This is almost always spoken in response to someone who would dare suggest that God's Law is everlasting (as the Bible says), that God requires proof of sanctification by way of behavior (as the Bible says), or that we are to be holy as He is holy (as the Bible says). While God is love, this is only stated in Scripture twice; the fact that God is holy or that He is connected to all holiness is used 620 times in Scripture. The "God of love" mantra is very simply another form of pride as man creates god in his own image, a safer, kinder model of god; new, and improved from that mean and nasty God of the Old Testament; a god who finally got saved and became "a Christian like us!!!!"

And, as stated earlier, this is all based on defining love apart from God's Biblical definition and from ignoring His Word as it regards love. When it is said, "I have a God of love" make no doubt about it, it is being stated that God cannot be love and law simultaneously and that law cannot be a part of love. In keeping with the ignorant fear of many of the "Old Testament" let us follow only the New Testament in our answer to Satan and those who follow his lead in "love."

Let us first hear from Jesus, the Son of God, and his opinion of law. Matthew 7:21-23 states, "Not everyone who says to Me, 'Lord, Lord,' will enter the kingdom of heaven, but he who does the will of My Father who is in heaven will enter. Many will say to Me on that day, 'Lord, Lord, did we not prophesy in Your name, and in Your name cast out demons, and in Your name perform many miracles?'
And then I will declare to them, 'I never knew you; depart from Me, you who practice lawlessness." We see Jesus speaking here of works of power and word, and finally, of relationship and banishment. The King James Version uses "iniquity" as the final word of the passage. The word in the Greek is *anomia*; "*a*" being "the lack of", and "*nomia*" the word for "law"; best translated "lawlessness." In other words, Jesus equates not knowing Him and He not knowing me with no law, the very opposite of those who have created the pandering "God of love."

Matthew 24:12 states, "Because lawlessness is increased, most people's love will grow cold..." For our purposes here the context of the verse does not matter as much as what is being said: "When lawlessness increases, love decreases"—a thought in direct opposition to those who equate a loving God with a lawless God.

In John 15:9-10 Jesus states, "Just as the Father has loved Me, I have also loved you; abide in My love. If you keep My commandments, you will abide in My love; just as I have kept My Father's commandments and abide in His love." Here Jesus equates abiding in His love and the Father's love with "keeping" (Greek = *tereo*) His commandments and Father's commandments. As stated earlier, the word "keep" does not mean obey, but has the strong connotation of meditation. Either way, Jesus is again equating law with love. Biblically and spiritually they are inseparable.

In I John 2:7-8, we read, "Beloved, I am not writing a new commandment to you, but an old commandment which you have had from the beginning; the old commandment is the word which you have heard. On the other hand, I am writing a new commandment to you, which is true in Him and in you, because the darkness is passing away and the true Light is already shining." The "new" commandment to love is not new. Jesus gives this new commandment in John 13:34 "A new commandment I give to you, that you love one another, even as I have loved you, that you also love one another. Jesus actually said little that was "new." When Jesus said that He was giving us a new commandment to love as He loved, He was defining love as in Romans 13:10 "Love does no wrong to a neighbor; therefore love is the fulfillment of the law." Love is the fulfillment of the law; but in the same way, the fulfillment of the law is love. Law is defined by love and love is defined by law. And note how John defines the "old commandment." He says, the old commandment is one "which you have had from the beginning"—the old commandments of God. But he also says that the old commandment is actually the new commandment. They are one and the same. The "old commandment" of law is the same as the new commandment of love.

The key to the new commandment is not to love as the law demanded; that was not new. Our cursory reading and rejection of the Old Testament has left us thinking so. If the fulfillment of the law is love, then the point of it all has always been love. The key to the "new commandment" is the phrase "as I have loved you." I cannot love as He loves; only He can love as He loves. His life must be in me to love as He loves. "It is no longer I who live, but Christ lives in me." The fulfillment of the law is what Christ came to do. That has not changed. He continues to fulfill the law within me—and that fulfillment is known as "love." Do not think that Jesus came and lived a perfect life by fulfilling the law, so you can do as you wish? His life in a believer does not stop fulfilling the law, because the new commandment is the old. The law defines love; love is the fulfillment of the law. The old commandment is the new; the new is the old.

But, His life and death did not cancel the law. Matthew 5:17-18 "Do not think that I came to abolish the Law or the Prophets; I did not come to abolish but to fulfill. For truly I say to you, until heaven and earth pass away, not the smallest letter or stroke shall pass from the Law until all is accomplished." All has not been accomplished. Heaven and earth have not passed away. I know there are those who would say that when Jesus said, "It is finished" on the cross that all was accomplished. What was finished was His redemption of you and me; not the cancellation of the Law of God. God is unchanging. Scripture describes His law as perfect, a delight, truth, something to be loved, the embodiment of knowledge and truth, spiritual and good. Paul stated in Romans that the "Law is holy, and the commandment is holy and righteous and good" and "that the requirement of the Law might be fulfilled in us, who do not walk according to the flesh but according to the Spirit." The simplicity of Paul's argument in his letters was not that the Law of God has been done away, but that our weak and arrogant attempts to obey that Law were of no avail in producing justification or righteousness; I am undone; nothing good dwells within me. I must rely on the life of Christ in me to live the Christian life.

But the requirements of living that life have not changed. The requirements of the Law are now fulfilled in me through Christ. And the requirements of the Law are defined by Christ and Paul in Scripture as "love." Some may quickly quote that we are not under law, but under grace. While that is absolutely true, God never intended for us to be "under law" as we have done. "Under law" is a man made condition which demands I obey the law to be righteous and justified before God. This was never taught in the Bible, as all of the covenants of God have been covenants of faith. "Abraham believed God and it was reckoned to him as righteousness." If that sounds like the gospel, it is because it is. Grace is not my excuse to live as I want. According to Romans 6:14 sin (defined Biblically as a violation of the law) shall not be master over you, for you are not under law but under grace. Grace is the power given to me to not be mastered by violations of the law. The law was given to define sin and to show my need of a Savior; it was never intended to bring justification or righteousness. Grace is the power to overcome sin, not my excuse to sin. Grace brings about righteousness, but righteousness is defined by law.

It would be easy (and arguably accurate) to say that the New Covenant which Christ brought about is grace. But we must define our terms accurately. Grace, if it defines the New Covenant, must be defined in terms of that covenant. And to restate that covenant, whether from Jeremiah 31 or Hebrews 8 and 10, it still reads, "I will put My laws upon their heart, and on their mind I will write them."

The law was not removed by the new covenant, but has actually drawn nearer, in fact, placed inside the partaker of that covenant. Grace, Biblically, is far removed from the compromised view of simply a free pass to heaven or the right to do whatever you wish because you are "saved by grace."

Obviously, there must be some point to this chapter, especially in relation to the subject of this book. And it is to give a Biblically based answer to the imagined quandary of law versus love. There is no separation or clash between law and love. The "God of love" is a "God of law."

Scripture states time and time again that it is those who keep His commandments that love Him. Repeating again John 14:21 "He who has My commandments and keeps them is the one who loves Me; and he who loves Me will be loved by My Father, and I will love him and will disclose Myself to him." I John 2:4-5 states, "The one who says, 'I have come to know Him,' and does not keep His commandments, is a liar, and the truth is not in him; but whoever keeps His word, in him the love of God has truly been perfected..."

Sin is the separator of God and man. God's answer to that separation was the substitutionary death of His sinless Son for that sin. I, the sinner, who was separated from God by my sin, have been brought near again to God by mercy and grace through the death of Jesus. The God of love has answered the God of Law.

But His answer was not to do away with the Law. His invitation to man is to draw near—for relationship. Messiah has closed the gap of sin which separated me from God. It is not the Law which separates me from God; it is my violation of that Law. Jesus did not die to cancel the Law.

He died because I violated the Law. And it is Law which defines sin (a violation of the Law) and it is Law which defines love ("keep" My commandments). As Paul states in Romans 6, "What shall we say then? Are we to continue in sin so that grace may increase? May it never be! How shall we who died to sin still live in it."

When I love someone, my desire is to be close to them and to avoid being separated from them. I avoid those things that would separate me from them and do things to bring me close to them. In the case of my heavenly Father it is sin (the violation of the Law) which separates me from Him; and it is keeping His commandments (listening to His Law, His nature) which keeps me close to Him. It is the same with human relationships. If I violate God's Law in relationship to them—hatred, anger, stealing, jealousy, adultery—it separates me from them. If I keep God's Law in relationship to them—patience, kindness, giving, love, loyalty—these keep me in closer relationship to them.

It is loving behavior which preserves relationship—whether with God or with man. That loving behavior must be one of two things: lawful or unlawful. It cannot be both. And loving behavior is defined by God's Law; not by violating that Law.

I John 2:5 states that "whoever keeps His Word, in him the love of God has truly been perfected." And later, in the fifth chapter of the same book it states, "By this we know that we love the children of God, when we love God and observe (*tereo*) His commandments. For this is the love of God, that we keep His commandments." The perfecting of God's love comes from "keeping" (meditating on) His Word, and to love His children I must love God and observe His commandments.

But, if I am to love as He loved, if I truly have a "God of love," I cannot get away from the fact that God defines that love by His Law. And it is only His Law, written on the belief system of my heart which will result in the love of God being perfected in me. To love God I must "keep" His commandments. To love others I must "keep" His commandments. "For this is the love of God, that we keep His commandments, and His commandments are not burdensome." God loves you. He is the God of love—in fact He is love. But the question must be asked: Do you love Him as He has stated you must, by "keeping" His commandments? God loves you, but He desires that you love His law. And in keeping His law you love Him and you love others. There is **no** other way.

In John 14:24 Jesus said, "He who does not love me does not keep my words…" We have two choices: love God or not love God. He says loving Him is keeping His word, specifically His commandments. He says not loving Him is not keeping His word. The question remains the same: Do you love God in the only way He has stated to love Him—by "keeping" His commandments?

Chapter 13
"Let's Not be Legalistic"

Any advertisement or propaganda campaign must contain words or phrases that create pictures in one's mind that illicit certain emotions. Christians are never "followers of Jesus Christ," they are "fundamentalists" or "radical religionists"; those that are pro-life are "anti-abortion forces" liberals are "progressives"; an emotional appeal is a "diatribe" or "rhetoric." These words, with the desired response, pass through our thoughts with such rapidity that we never really notice the subtle shift in our beliefs. We as humans are so confident that we make our decisions and form opinions only from faultless logic that we have become glassy-eyed poultry, simply waiting for the next emotional counterfeit of the truth. And we as Christians are so confident in our "grace" covered, saved state, that our every individual thought, word, and feeling must come directly from the Throne of God itself, that we openly welcome as truth serpentine wisdom in rejecting the innocence of the dove. We have come to believe—not that we have ever thought we believed it—that our catchwords and phrases are simply truth and our enemy, the father of propagandas, cannot invade our holy fortress. (Jesus, Paul, and Peter must have been mistaken when they urged us to be always on the alert!)

Satan has quietly and ever so slowly anesthetized the church with false suppositions which have insidiously become accepted as truth—and just as insidiously have spread by mouth through the body—weakening it in the two areas which must be singularly upheld to distinguish the church from the world surrounding it: unwavering truth and holiness. We have slowly accepted these ideas as the body would accept a virus, fooled into believing that these words are actually a "deeper, more humane" approach to the truth and will undoubtedly bring good. (Haven't we heard it before? "You surely shall not die...but your eyes will be opened...")

One of these words has become so commonly used, has such a ring of "tolerance, and freedom" that it is found in seemingly every Christian's vocabulary, is heard at least once in every doctrinal discussion and many sermons, and is so powerful that it is the final word of doctrinal arguments, immediately placing those to whom it addressed into a dulled stupor of shamed agreement.

Yet, it is not a word ever spoken by the Lord Jesus, Moses, Paul, or David. In fact, it is not in the Bible at all. Those, who through the centuries have been tortured, imprisoned, and martyred for the Faith, would have not even understood its lofty but hollow concept. While not in the Bible itself, this word is used most often to negate or combat another word which is very often found in the Bible and is at the foundational core of the Christian's understanding of such concepts as "Lord," "King," "Master," "Ruler," and "all authority." That word is "obedience." It is an uncomfortable word, a word which not only threatens My Kingdom, but guarantees its destruction, and, as such, must be defended against and rendered a void term. To combat this annoying idea of true obedience to God, Satan has supplied us with a shelter into which we plunge with much relief—the narcotic word "legalism," which is our focus here. I have written this chapter because one can already hear the wailing, and gnashing of teeth from those who would follow any doctrine if it left them with no responsibility except empty but comfortable, ear and ego tickling religion.

We desperately and purposefully scuttle the fact that

obedience to God and His Word (He considers Himself and His Word as the same entity, John 1:1) is one of the major themes of the Bible. Have we lost the understanding that He is Creator and we are the created; that He is to be honored, obeyed, and glorified—not I? That we were created for His pleasure, not He for ours? Yet we are so quick to discount anyone who dares suggest that we are to obey that which we see in Scripture, or who speaks a particular Biblical principle that if violated will have certain promised consequences. And the word which is used most often to thwart the innocent inquiry of obedience is legalism.

The first problem with the use of the term "legalism" is that it is more of an undefined concept rather than a concrete term, its "definition" vague and therefore its application broad. As such, it can set up its standard at any point, "draw the line" wherever convenient. But even if we shore up the concept with definition, its application into Christian life is out of place. Webster's New Collegiate Dictionary defines legalism as "a strict, literal, or excessive conformity to the law or to religious or moral code." If we accept this definition (especially when focusing on "strict, literal") we certainly find who is truly legalistic—GOD!! One of the biggest complaints against Judeo-Christianity is "all those do's and don'ts" and even a casual reader of the Bible knows that He appears to be rather insistent on our obeying those do's and don'ts. It gets worse, of course, when we realize that God not only insists on "strict and literal conformity to the law," but He is actually the Author of the law. Some would have us believe that the God of the Old Testament realized His mistake with this law and obedience thing He was pushing, changed His mind, changed His being, and stepped into a nearby phone booth and emerged as the "new and improved" God of the New Testament, free from those troubling hang-ups of commandments, laws, and obedience with which He had so struggled. Neither the Old Testament nor the New mentions such an idea. Isaiah 40: 8 states, "The grass withers, the flower fades, but the word of our God stands forever." Malachi 3: 6 tells us "For I, the Lord, do not change...." Hebrews 13: 8 states, "Jesus Christ, the same yesterday, today, and forever." In Matthew 5: 17-18 Jesus tells us, "Do not think I came to abolish the Law or the Prophets; I did not come to abolish but to fulfill. For truly I say to you, until heaven and earth pass away, not the smallest letter or stroke shall pass away from the law until all is accomplished." All has not been accomplished; heaven and earth are still here; Jesus doesn't change; God is unchanging; the Word stands forever—The God of the Old Testament is the God of the New. His insistence on obedience to His Law has been answered by Jesus' perfect obeying of that Law for us. But, this substitution, this grace is for our freedom to obey His will—not for our freedom to disobey as we wish. Ah, but wait—the definition states also "excessive conformity." That's it! It's the excessive conformity that irritates us so. But really, our objections become more pitifully weak (no matter how we may shout them!) with a simple look at conformity. To conform is to "be of the same form." Scripture tells us that we are to "become conformed to the image of His Son" (Rom. 8:29). How can we actively be seeking and desiring to be like Christ and at the same time be actively seeking and desiring to not be excessively like Christ? How does one set up a standard as that to which he will strive to attain, but simultaneously work to not get too close to the standard? We actually have become more fearful of doing something righteous or approving of something righteous than fearing coming close to evil and compromise. No wonder those outside the church focus on our flagrant hypocrisy and mock at the foolishness our "life in Christ" has become.

And if we continue to state that obedience to certain parts of God's Word is legalism, which parts do we retain to obey and which parts do we not obey? Where do we draw the line that obedience ends and legalism begins? How "close" do we get to evil before we say our actions are not legalism? Or how far do we get from righteousness before we are not legalistic? This whole concept is rather preposterous, or should be, to the Christian who claims to follow Christ. The real question to pose to those prone to label others as legalistic is not what actions they define as legalistic, but rather what actions they have decided are not legalism! If we are allowed to draw this line where we wish, we certainly will draw it for our own convenience. Of course, the real problem comes with the fact that we believe we can draw the line at all. For if the line can be drawn arbitrarily, cannot someone say that it is legalism to believe that Jesus is the only way to eternal life, that one must be born again, that one must be baptized, that we should participate in Communion, that we must believe Jesus is the Son of God? And why can we not simply throw out that silliness about the cross and resurrection and remission of sins with the rest of what we consider trite or inconvenient? Remember, we are commanded by God to believe these things—but if obeying God's commandments is legalism—well; we don't want to be legalistic.

The Book of Judges (17:6; 21:25) tells us twice that God's people were constantly under judgment because they "did what was right in their own eye." How are we different than they if we decide on our own what words of Scripture we will obey and what we won't, what I think applies to my life as opposed to what I consider "legalistic"?

Certainly these are all rhetorical questions. But they do have an answer: We want no one, including God, setting up a standard of behavior for us that we cannot lower, remove, or negate—which, of course, leaves all standard setting up to us as individuals and must eventually result in no standard of behavior since every standard established shifts or disappears at our will. Therefore, if we do believe that there is good and evil, light and darkness, truth and lies, righteousness and sin—where do we get these beliefs? And who says what sin is and what is not? We certainly did not get these beliefs from ourselves. Our selfish, murderous ways certainly nullify that notion. The fact is, of course, that the true standard of behavior comes from God in His Word, Who does not change, nor does His standard of righteousness change; for it is not we, but God, the Father, the Son, or the Holy Spirit Who defines sin. A quick look at the book of Romans lets us know that the standard of righteousness and sin has not changed—it remains God's Moral Law. Romans 7:7, "What shall we say then? Is the Law sin? May it never be!! On the contrary, I would not have come to know sin except through the Law..."; 3:20 "...for through the Law comes the knowledge of sin"; 5:13: "...sin is not imputed where there is no law neither is there violation."; 4:5: "but where there is no law neither is there violation."; 6:16: "Do you not know that when you present yourselves to someone as slaves for obedience, you are slaves of the one whom you obey, either of sin resulting in death, or obedience resulting in righteousness?" We have already seen that Jesus has stated that the entire Law stands until heaven and earth pass away. And, if that is so, then doing even the smallest "jot or tittle" of God's Word and Will is not legalism but righteous behavior. And to label obedience or a desire of obedience to God as "legalism" is not righteousness but compromise.

Perhaps we should quickly look at other definitions of legalism rather than simply the authoritative one from a dictionary. Because, you see, as already stated, while the term legalism rings with authority and strength, it actually has no true jurisdiction or single definition. Its definition changes as its user has need, and its jurisdiction covers all standards of behavior except its own— that of judging others.

There are times that our chameleonic catchword assumes the definition of "earning salvation by the works of the law;" in other words, trusting in your own goodness for salvation rather than Jesus' sacrifice, righteousness, and grace. Galatians 2:16, as well as the entire Bible, warns against this: "nevertheless, knowing that a man is not justified by the works of the Law but through faith in Christ Jesus that we may be justified by faith in Christ, and not by works of the Law; since by the works of the Law shall no flesh be justified." It is obvious that if one is attempting to be justified before God on his own righteous behavior that it will not work! And if this is legalism, it is certainly wrong in God's eyes. But, the question now must be "Is this legalism?" It certainly does not match our dictionary definition. And as we must admit, Scripture does not call it legalism, because it never uses the word. The book of Galatians does label such action with other terms such as transgressor (2:18), bewitched (3:1), cursed (3:10), severed from Christ (5:4), and fallen from grace (5:4). If this is a spiritual problem should we not use a spiritual, Biblical word for its label? And at least something that is precise and uniform, rather than self-defined and fluctuating. So while this behavior and belief may be many things, and, in fact, so many wrong things that it cannot be included in the realm of true

Christianity, it cannot be accurately called legalism.

But even apart from its non-Biblical origin there are other problems with this definition. The vast majority of the time, when the term legalism is used, it is applied to Christians. I have known and been known by thousands of Christians in my life, and no matter how poor their grasp of the gospel and doctrine and the Bible, not one has ever expressed to me that their ultimate hope for salvation was not truly and only in Jesus Christ . Many were those whose doctrine and salvation some might question, but the fact remains, their hope was in Christ, not in their own righteousness or works. There may be those that call themselves Christian that do not hope in Jesus—but I have met none when truly pressed for their beliefs. But if these exist they really fit into the category of people who believe the "good Lord over looks our faults, and I've lived a good life." They're not legalistic—they are lost!

This same argument would continue to hold true even if we again change the definition. (This word is so convenient!) . So, we now will give the definition of "trying to live the Christian life on our own strength without relying on the grace of God and Christ in us." Again, this is certainly the wrong way to live as a Christian and must end (and begin) in failure, and the previous arguments apply here also. But it is not legalism! It is pride (Eph. 2:8,"... not as a result of works that no one should boast."); it is foolish (Gal. 3:3, "...are you now being perfected by the flesh?"); and it is many other things—but it is not legalism.

A closer look at the way legalism is used reveals another interesting flaw in its use: the use of the term is actually the height of hypocrisy. Those that use the term are usually objecting to the fact that some standard of behavior has been set before them. Yet, their use of the term "legalism" is their setting a certain standard (usually lower) for another person's behavior! They are setting a standard against setting a standard! So, we have one Christian who says, "I believe that we are saved by grace and not works, and to me the standard of righteous behavior is obedience to God's word." And the reply from another Christian is this, "I believe we are saved by grace and not by works, but to me the standard of righteous behavior is not obeying God's Word because that would be legalism." Sound confusing? It should! Think about it. One person's excuse for obeying God's Word is because they love Him; and another person's excuse for disobeying Him is because they love Him!

Let us look more closely at the concepts of salvation and righteous behavior. We have already established that the standard of righteous behavior for the Christian must come only from God's Word and cannot come from what each person may deem right in his own mind or what he thinks he hears in his spirit. Therefore, God's law is the standard for right and wrong. And mankind has proven over and over that he will not hold to that standard. And, as such, he cannot make himself righteous or become righteous by working the works of God's Law. Only failure and frustration await the one who would attempt obeying the Law to gain salvation. But if that Law is not the standard by which we are judged, then why would Jesus have to die for us? The entire concept of Christianity must rest upon a righteous standard of behavior established by a righteous God. Anything otherwise negates any reason for Jesus' death on the cross. Therefore, Romans 10:9-10 states that "if you confess with your mouth Jesus as Lord, and believe in your heart that God raised Him from the dead, you shall be saved; for with the heart man believes, resulting in righteousness, and with the mouth he confesses, resulting in salvation." Certainly there is nothing about working our way into salvation there, and it is clear our righteousness comes only from believing in Jesus' righteousness. Ephesians 2: 8-10 speaks with even more preciseness regarding our salvation through faith and not works, but adds a charge to that truth that is a result of that salvation. Listen carefully to the words that describe not only our salvation by faith alone but what is to be our response to that salvation: "For by grace you have been saved through faith; and that not of yourselves, it is the gift of God; not as a result of works, that no one should boast; For we are His workmanship, created in Christ Jesus for good works, which God prepared beforehand, that we should walk in them." Again, adamantly, we are saved by grace alone and never by our own works. We are new creatures, created in Christ Jesus. But for what are we created? For "good works"—not for avoiding good works because we or someone else may brand us "legalistic"! Not to walk as close to compromise as we can, so we may appear to be accepting and tolerant of the world (we are to be neither). And not doing the actions we judge to be good works. It is only God who can tell us what His good works are. We have already established that we cannot do so--because man has shown (and we as individuals have shown) that we will rationalize the most vile atrocities as what is "right in our own eyes," and I certainly will label as "good" any charitable, kindly, or churchly act that may feed the bottomless pit of my disguised ego and pride. Therefore, we must have only one standard of what is good and that can only be God's opinion—which is His Word. And if we are saved for good works, and those good works are defined in God's Word, then how dare we fear or label as legalistic the very things which do show us to be followers of Jesus and markedly different from the world.

If the same spirit of persecution of believers of the first century was operating in the United States today, the Coliseum would run out of victims after the first weekend. How would they know whom to persecute? The Church now has the world's entertainment, the world's music, the world's methods, the world's words, the world's prophets and teachers, the world's books, the world's philosophies, the world's counselors, the world's morals—all having been made much more palatable by an inability to confront evil created by the fear of appearing legalistic. In fact, we have begun to work harder at not appearing legalistic than in any pursuit of appearing righteous. The Lord tells us we are to seek first His righteousness, not first seek to appear free from legalism. Righteousness is "right with God," doing things His way, not ours. Romans 6 : 16 states, "Do you not know that when you present yourselves to someone as slaves for obedience you are slaves of the one whom you obey either of sin resulting in death or of obedience resulting in righteousness?" It is <u>obedience</u> that results in <u>righteousness</u>—not our attempts to escape it. It is not to gain salvation from God that we owe Him righteousness, but rather it is that we owe God righteousness because we have gained salvation from Him. While some may say obedience is legalism and is attempting to work your way into the kingdom of heaven, the counter is that obedience is actually the kingdom of heaven working its way into you.

In Scripture we only see righteousness and sin, not righteousness, sin, and legalism. The Garden of Eden did not contain the tree of the knowledge of good and evil and legalism. God's good works, what He views as righteous are <u>not</u> legalistic but holy and just, to be embraced as the reason and result for our salvation, not shunned for fear of appearing too righteous!! For while we cannot be made righteous by obeying the Law, we are certainly made unrighteous by not obeying it. And it is when we fail to obey His Law that we have entered "the unrighteous." "Blessed are those who are persecuted for the sake of righteousness," not for the sake of unrighteousness or compromise in the face of the fear of being "too" righteous. Scripture is constant in its call for us to ere on the side of "too much righteousness" (how can there be such a thing) rather than not enough righteousness. When Christ used as a standard the most "legalistic" men of His time, He said, "...Unless your righteousness surpasses that of the scribes and Pharisees you shall not enter the kingdom of heaven." (Matthew 5:20) The compromised are never accused of legalism. Those that are attempting to fully embrace God's ways and laws suffer the reviling word legalism—not those that embrace compromise to avoid earthly discomfort.

And the greatest of those earthly discomforts is really at the base of this entire argument—the subjugation of our wills. This is the problem from Genesis to Revelation—who is the Creator and who is the created? Who is Master and who is servant? Who is the "no other God before Me" and who is the object of loving with all our heart, soul, and might? It is interesting that these basic ideas involve a clash of wills. And that clash of wills is measured by the standard of one thing—obedience. Will it be obedience to me, my will and my word, or obedience to God, His will, and His Word? My obedience is not to prove who is righteous and who is not, but rather obedience is to prove who is God and who is not.

In I Samuel 15 King Saul is doing something good— he is sacrificing to God. Well, it would have been good but for one thing. He had to disobey God to do it. He was doing something which in his own eyes was good but was not the way God had stated it should be done. The prophet Samuel then reminds us all that doing something for God (i.e., "sacrificing ourselves"), which we think is good, is not as important as simple obedience to God. "To obey is better than sacrifice." Why is this so? The sacrificial laws of the Old Testament are very specific for good reason. If we didn't have specific instructions, our wills would dictate what or how much we sacrificed, and relegate God to our creation rather than we His. And do not think such instructions are lacking in the New Testament. "Beware of practicing your righteousness before men in such a way as to be noticed by them... Do not give, pray, or fast so as to be noticed by men. We as humans have not changed through the centuries. Sacrifice can involve what I want—obedience only involves what God wants. Sacrifice involves giving something up—obedience involves our will. Obedience is better than sacrifice because obedience is placing our will under His.

So we see that often our "sacrifices" to the Lord are more precisely sacrifices to our egos presented in the temple of our own will. Our obedience to God is not to His Word, His Will (the very word "testament" means "will"), but is rather obedience to a "feeling" that we equate to being "led by the Spirit." And it is amazing how quickly we may obey those "feelings" even though they may be in direct violation of His Word! I've heard a pastor say, "I know what the Bible says about borrowing money, but that's not where I'm at." A woman we were counseling, when told there was no Scriptural grounds for the divorce she was planning screamed, "I don't believe that!" And I know of a deacon board chairman, when asked by his pastor if they would handle a situation Biblically, "The Bible doesn't work!" The stories are endless. So, in today's church doctrine we have God's Word opposing His Will and God's direction determined by individual abdominal pain. It has come to a point that we must "feel" we are lead to obey any of the Lord's words. If we "feel" we are being "led" to obey, it won't be legalism, but will be honored as being "led by the Spirit." And this is precisely where again "legalism" attacks obedience to God. Amazingly we lay aside any pursuit of righteousness that we may not offend Him by appearing legalistic. It sounds so good: "God, I am so resting in your righteousness that I will no longer pursue righteousness, but will do only the right thing if I feel you are leading me to do. If I obey Your Word I might appear legalistic, so I set that aside to be led only as I feel You lead me." While we do not hear these specific words, our heart and attitudes scream them.

Jesus Christ paid a most terrible price for our lack of obedience. The price of our lack of obedience was Christ's death; the price of Christ's death should be our obedience.

Jesus said in Matthew 7, "Not everyone who says to Me, 'Lord, Lord' will enter the kingdom of heaven; but he who does the will of My Father Who is in heaven. Many will say to Me on that day, 'Lord, Lord, did we not prophesy in Your name, and in Your name cast out demons, and in Your name perform many miracles? And then I will declare to them, 'I never knew you; Depart from Me you who practice lawlessness.' " These are among the strongest words spoken to confront ME at my perceived bases of power. The first perceived base of power is the spoken word. The belief that if "I" benevolently acknowledge with my mouth Jesus as Lord the state of my obedience to His will is secondary to those words, when the opposite is the real truth. My doing His will is the only thing that will give substance to my calling Him "*Lord*." And the placement of professing before performing violates not only the letter but the spirit of not using the Lord's name in a vain way and of bearing false witness of who we are to Him and Who He is to us. To call Him "Lord" with our lips and disobey Him with our life is as false a witness as can be borne to "Jerusalem and in all Judea and Samaria and even to the remotest part of the earth." We take the name "Christian" in vain when we call Him Lord and do not listen to or obey His Word or when we teach that His law has been nullified.

The second base of power of ME is that of "busyness."—doing God's work, working for the Lord in His Name! It is interesting to observe that many of those that brand others as legalistic are the busiest doing "for Him" or learning "about Him," but rarely "learning Him." And this is precisely the point Jesus makes here. Our works in His name are not what He is seeking from us. He wants me. "...I never knew you." The word use for "knew" is the Greek word for "knowing completely" or "I never knew you, came to observe you as having experienced Me." (Complete Word Study Dictionary ,p. 374, Zodhiates). So here is the judgment on us when we work so hard in His name (and then are so bold as to tell God how much we have done for Him)—"Depart from Me!" He then adds the final characteristic of the "busy believers"—"...you who practice lawlessness." (The King James translates "ye that work iniquity.") The picture He gives us is so striking, because, as many of His teachings are, it is not as we would expect. He tells us these are so busy working for Him, they never spend time with Him; and then, while they call Him "Lord, Lord," they practice lawlessness. The Greek word here for lawlessness is anomia: "a"—without; and nomia—law, or "not having, knowing, or acknowledging the Law." (Complete Word Study Dictionary, p. 186-187). In other words, He, Jesus, the Son of God, the Word of God, equates not being known by Him with <u>not</u> <u>knowing</u> <u>or</u> <u>acknowledging</u> <u>the</u> <u>Law</u>!! "Depart from Me! I never knew you, you who say there is no law!" What a terrible, frightening contrast to those that would tell us we are <u>free</u> from the Law! From those that would tell us not to be legal! "Depart from Me! I never knew you; you who say don't be legalistic!"

We in today's church have become so compromised with the world that we can no longer use God's Law as a standard of righteousness. Not only because we can scarcely recognize it for lack of use but also because we are so busy being "free" from it, we have had to invent a make believe sin—legalism. We condemn the righteous for their righteousness—and applaud the compromised as truly free in Christ. Romans 6: 15-16: "What then? Shall we sin because we are not under law but under grace? May it never be! Do you not know that when you present yourselves to someone as slaves for obedience, you are slaves to one whom you obey, either of sin resulting in death, or of obedience resulting in righteousness?" Christ has set us free <u>from</u> sin, not free <u>to</u> sin!

Legalism is never listed as a sin in Scripture—it is one of those modern church sins. But the use of this term is a real sin, that of being judgmental. The real reason we want to set our own standard of righteousness is to justify ourselves. Therefore, when we call another person legalistic for their standard, we are attempting to justify <u>our</u> <u>own</u> standard and behavior—the very thing we are accusing the other person of doing. And Paul's words from Romans 2 : 1 ring true through all time, "...every man of you who passes judgment, for in that you judge another you condemn yourself; you who judge practice the same things."

And here I will finally add that I do understand that Scripture is very clear that "obedience" from the flesh is not desired by our Lord. But, this book has been very clear that Scripture also tells us that "keeping" God's Word in our heart through meditation changes the belief system which changes outward behavior—all by His grace and the power of His Holy Spirit.

But why bring this up in a book on relationship with God? We are to be in right relationship with God. My sin, iniquity, and transgression separate me from God, not my legalism. The fear of legalism has become an excuse for sin that is inexcusable. Put aside your Satan-bred fear of being "too holy" or of "appearing too good." We are to walk in the fear of the Lord, not the fear of legalism. This concept of fearing righteousness is one of the biggest impediments ever designed by God's enemy to keep us from intimacy with our heavenly Father—and enslaved to the enemy of our soul.

CHAPTER 14
In The Spirit of Holiness

I have already spoken of my problems with anger and lack of relationship with God, but sin in general had a strong grip on my life. It did not matter what sin: anger, lust, greed, selfishness, pride; they all could manifest themselves in my life at what seemed to be their will. When I first began to memorize and meditate on Scripture, it was out of the sheer desperation that nothing seemed to be right in my "Christian" life.

But the first thing to happen was not something I could have predicted. I unexpectedly began to have victory over sins which had owned me for many years. You know the one in your life. You can see it coming; you can feel it coming. No matter how strongly you purpose to be good/nice/chaste/honest/ caring, failure is waiting for you, and you rush toward it like an out of control train toward a gaping gorge—there is no bridge. You can apply non-existent brakes, plead for it to stop, and close your eyes—you still fall to its power. But the surprise ending came. Closed-eyed and braced for the fall, I found I had passed a strong temptation without the smallest bump in the way. When the same scene had repeated itself enough times for me to suspect that something beyond my power to resist temptation was at work, I asked the Lord for the reason for my newly realized power over sin. He answered immediately with a Scripture verse which I had not thought of often since my childhood: "Thy Word have I hid in my heart that I might not sin against Thee." (Psalm 119:11)

A simple verse which says much; God's Word is hidden; God's Word is hidden in my heart (my belief system) not just my brain. My heart is the seat of my belief system, where I really believe, where behavior originates. It is where the King of my life tells me what to do; my obedience only depends on who is King. But it is not just that the word is in my heart; it is hidden there. The 13th chapter of Matthew is the "Kingdom of Heaven" chapter. It contains seven of Jesus' parables, all of them about the kingdom of heaven. And all of them have one thing in common—something is hidden. Seeds, leaven, treasure, pearls, fish in the sea are all hidden until revealed as the kingdom. The first of these parables (and according to Mark 4:13 the one which we must understand to understand all other parables) tells us what is hidden—The Word. Something hidden is not seen. Faith is the evidence of things not seen (Hebrews 11:1). Romans 10:17 tells us that faith comes from hearing and hearing by the Word of God. The point is obvious— God's Word must be heard and hidden in our hearts. Reading it, hearing a sermon or teaching will not do. It must go deeper. It must be hidden. And it is hidden through meditation.

When it is hidden it does its work as a seed planted in the ground. Belief equates to behavior; but it must be the belief hidden in the heart. And it is when the Word of God is hidden in my heart that I agree with God—and do not sin against Him.

Have you ever wondered at Isaiah 40:3 which says, "A voice is calling, clear the way for the Lord in the wilderness; make smooth in the desert a highway for our God." Does our all powerful God need me, the weak human, to clear a path for Him to physically get around? I think not. The issue is the twisted path of my belief system, in rebellion and disagreement with Him. Later, in Isaiah 55: 8 he states, "For My thoughts are not your thoughts, nor are your ways My ways." I have often heard these verses used to show

how far removed God is from man. But if you look closely at the context you will see that God is not putting us in our place—He is rebuking us for not coming up to His place—holiness!!

You see it is sin that separates me from God. This is stated over and over in Scripture. It is that separation caused by sin which so concerns God. Sin is the opposite of His nature. Therefore, it must separate me from Him. We have tried to make the issue that sin is so hideous to God because He is so holy. I am not arguing against God's holiness; I am actually trying to define it Biblically. It is interesting that sin is separation from God, and the term "holy" in Scripture, whether Greek or Hebrew, means "separate, apartness." God is separate from the world's system, very separate. He did not invent it or invite it. His ways are higher. But His invitation to those in covenant with Him is to be holy, to be separate from the world's system and its perversion of all that is good. It is not God's holiness that separates Him from man; it is man's sin that separates him from God. That is the reason God hates sin. And that is the reason for the death of Jesus on the cross. Jesus was holy, wholly separated unto the Father. When He died, I died, because, as Paul states, all died in Christ. But now that I have been raised in Him I live in Him. Since it is no longer I who live, but Christ, I can finally answer God's statement of fact: "You are holy, because I am holy." He did not say I was to act holy. I cannot do so. The fact is that because I am in Christ, in covenant with God, I am separate from the world as He is. I belong to Him, not to another and not to self.

My separateness (holiness) from the world begins with that question—who is my king, who owns me? I have been bought with a price. I am no longer my own—but especially in one hidden area I rarely consider. And that is the subject here—the before-mentioned belief system in my heart. I belong to God. His belief system is holy; my belief system should be His belief system, holy. His belief system is His Word. But, even with the correct belief system, I need another power to exercise that belief system in the real world. That power is the Holy Spirit. Man, without God is nothing more than a beast. God has supplied (and is Himself) the mode of closest relationship and cooperation— His very life within us: the Holy Spirit. And if we would but listen to the title of His Spirit we would better understand His function: **HOLY** Spirit. The Holy Spirit fills me and lives in me; better stated, He lives me. Paul stated it this way, "It is no longer I who live, but Christ lives in me." The same Holy Spirit that empowered Jesus Christ to live a perfect and blameless life for me now lives in me!!! The same Holy Spirit who wrote the Bible with God's Holy law (2 Peter 1:20-21) lives in me. Christ died, shed His perfect blood to grant me holiness and righteousness which I cannot do and do not deserve. His Holy Spirit then fills me to live holiness and righteousness which I cannot do and do not deserve. The true Christian life is **total** dependence on God through the power of the Holy Spirit.

We see the Holy Spirit's presence mentioned in all areas of the Bible, not just the New Testament (New Covenant). But there is a difference in the New Covenant. We see it in John the Baptist's statement at the baptism of Jesus in the first chapter of John, "John testified saying, 'I have seen the Spirit descending as a dove out of heaven, and He remained upon Him. I did not recognize Him, but He who sent me to baptize in water said to me, 'He upon whom you see the Spirit descending and remaining upon Him, this is the One who baptizes in the Holy Spirit.'" We then see

Jesus stating the same thing in John 14:16 "I will ask the Father, and He will give you another Helper, that He may be with you forever." The difference between the New Covenant and all other Biblical covenants is one thing: the Holy Spirit remains—forever. In the Old Testament we see the Holy Spirit moving on prophets—but He did not remain. The New Covenant is a better covenant. Jesus said in John 14:18 that he would not leave us as orphans while talking of the gift of the Holy Spirit. The Holy Spirit is Emmanuel—God with us.

But this same passage from John 14 has something of deep interest to the subject of meditation and "keeping" God's Word. If we add verse 15 we see the following connected thoughts: "If you love Me, you will keep My commandments and I will ask the Father, and He will give you another Helper, that He may be with you forever." Do you see it? Jesus tells us to love Him by "keeping" (meditating on) His commandments, and then connects that to the gift of the Holy Spirit. A few verses later He tells us in verses 25-26, "These things I have spoken to you while abiding with you. But the Helper, the Holy Spirit, whom the Father will send in My name, He will teach you all things, and bring to your remembrance all that I said to you." Again, He is promising the Holy Spirit, but what things had He just spoken? "He who has my commandments and keeps them he it is who loves me....If anyone loves me he will keep my word....He who does not love me does not keep my words...." He speaks of keeping the commandments, and then refers to the promise of the Holy Spirit to teach us (meditation) and bring to our remembrance what Jesus has said (memorization). Both passages connect keeping the commandments with the presence of the Holy Spirit.

And this makes perfect sense. If the Holy Spirit is to work within me, my mind and my heart must agree with Him. The Holy Spirit wrote the Law. It is holy. His purpose, like His title is holiness. But it is holiness for mankind—God is already holy. But, if He is to work through me, my belief system, my heart, must agree with Him. I cannot agree with His work of holiness in my life while at the same time disagreeing with His Word and not keeping it in my heart. In such a case, I would have the author of the holy law of God, the very Spirit of the God Who is separate from the world's system living in me, while disagreeing with Him in my heart. This is the reason that the first chapter of James tells us to "receive the Word implanted which is able to save your **soul** (not save my spirit). Sadly, this double-mindedness is the description of many of the lives of professing believers in Christ—a profession of "belief" with the mouth coupled with a belief system in the heart, which is completely inconsistent with the Words and belief system of God.

The life of a Christian—a life "like Christ"—cannot be lived without total dependence on the Holy Spirit to live that life for me. I have no power in myself to do so. As Paul states in Romans 7, "For I know that nothing good dwells in me, that is, in my flesh; for the willing is present in me, but the doing of the good is not. For the good that I want, I do not do, but I practice the very evil that I do not want." He concludes by the end of the chapter that the only thing that can save him from himself is the life of Christ—the Holy Spirit living in him.

Holiness is not putting on the correct clothes, with a correct haircut, with a correct demeanor, and a correct religion, and correct Bible version. These things may result from holiness, but they are not holiness. Holiness is my belonging to God, not to self. But that belonging must include what I think, what I meditate on, what I daydream about, what is hidden in my heart. Jesus said in Mark 4:24, "Take care what you listen to." His Word, hidden in my heart, agreeing with His Spirit living in my heart, will make me a person who not only does not sin against God, but does not desire to sin against God. The desire for a sanctified life is a fight and strain which weighs on all who love God; but that fight and strain teaches us to be totally dependent upon Him with our every breath. It is His Holy Spirit which empowers me to be His possession, His creature, His worshipper. And it is His Word, hidden in my heart, which brings my soul into agreement, and therefore my behavior into agreement with the life of God in me. The book of James says, "For we all stumble in many ways." We all have a "sin problem." But that sin problem will and must persist with great strength if what I believe in my heart, if what I have thought or heard until I believe, is inconsistent with God's Word. If I do not love Jesus Christ and the Father by "keeping" His Word through meditation, my life will bear out, not the life of a person given over to God, but rather a life which resoundingly says with the serpent of old, "Has God said?"

Chapter 15
Builders of Babel; Butchers of the Body
Or
Feed My Sheep
(The Call of Leadership)

If a relationship with God through meditation is as important as has been shown so far in this book, why do we not hear about it more in the church? There are a number of reasons, all which point back to the common enemy of all mankind—Satan.

Satan hates the Word of God. He is a liar and the Word is Truth. His first attack against man and God involved the Word: "Indeed, has God said…" His continued attacks are first against God's Word. Satan knows that for man to love God he must keep God's commandments. Therefore, his number one goal is to keep man from the commandments in God's Word.

One of his primary schemes to keep man from God's Word is so well camouflaged that even when exposed it is hard to believe such a thing could be true—he uses leadership in the church. It began long ago—at least as early as the Catholic Church's use of Latin and its incessant battles to keep the Word out of the hands of the common man. Many of the heroes of the faith were those who translated the Bible to put it into the hands of the believer. John Huss, William Tyndale, Martin Luther were men who lived and even died to bring God's Word to man. And do not think it is the Catholic Church who stands alone in guilt—all organized religion has something to do with the keeping of God's Word from man. Even those who boast in *Sola Scriptura* fall all over themselves to prove their theological points by appealing to Calvin, Luther, the Early Church Fathers, or unbiblical terms such as "irresistible grace" or defining the word "all" in Scripture to only mean "some." This is **not** *Sola Scriptura*!!! And the camp of Arminius is no better in its lack of Biblical approach. We all add man's wisdom and take from God's to achieve our ends.

Unfortunately, the perpetuation of man's kingdom (denominations) often overshadows the entry into God's Kingdom. Our seminaries are created to disseminate the denominational dogma—damn the Truth and full speed ahead if it gets in the way. We train our pastors to manipulate people rather than love them as Christ loves. Seminars on "church growth" (That's "your" church, not the other guys), manipulating your flock to give more money, training for "worship" services to appeal to emotions are no different in spirit than the Catholic indulgences that the Protestant movement protested against!!!

It is not and never has been about the church. Jesus did not come preaching, "Repent for the church is at hand." Our focus is to be on His Kingship—not our kingship. Our pastors and denominational leaders are in constant angry debates over things which matter little to those who are living and perishing in darkness. What a waste of time, intellect, and life our precious theologies are. The "church" is not an institution—it is the Bride of Christ. If she is so, then church leadership should stop treating her as their personal prositute, to use, abuse, manipulate, and seek personal glory in at our beckoned whim. The true church is not the organization we now see, so intent on being correct and separate from others; judging those who do not name the name of Christ like we name the name of Christ. The organized religious beast we have created is the architect that can proudly claim credit for finally finishing the Tower of Babel!!

Jesus prayed that those in Him would be ONE!!! WE ARE!!! When we travel, we find those who love us and each other, despite the Protestant Popes demanding the Dark Ages continue. You in Christ know this to be true—you fellowship with many who could not care less where you go to "church". Have I offended you yet? A better question is "Have you offended you yet?" Or have I offended me yet— with my lust for numbers on the rolls, my demand for my name being glorified, my insatiable appetite for being right and recognized for it, or my "church/denomination/theology-is-better-than-yours" attitude. Shame on us all!!! Satan incited crowds to crucify Christ; we incite them to butcher His Body.

Can you imagine a shepherd who would chew the grass for the sheep in his flock and spit it into their mouths? And that the reason for this behavior was that he, and the sheep, had been convinced that they were not qualified to chew grass? Yet, that is precisely what we have done in the church—we tell those in covenant with Christ, those that have been translated into His kingdom, those filled with the promise of the Holy Spirit that they cannot know the truth except when told them by a trained, professional religionist.

Jesus told us to make disciples. And in John 8:31 He defined a disciple as one who abides in His Word—not someone who must listen to one pastor or denomination, lest he be branded a heretic and rebel. We are to make disciples of Jesus Christ; not disciples of denominations, pastors, or popes. They are to follow His voice; they are to keep His commandments; they are to be His disciples—not mine. My job as a leader in the Kingdom of God is to work myself out of a job. I must not have people clinging to my every word and dependent on me. I am to train others to cling to God's Word and to be dependent on Him. My interpretation of His Word is not discipleship; discipleship is training others to listen to the Holy Spirit and abide in God's Word. Jesus said in John 14 that the Holy Spirit would "teach you all things, and bring to your remembrance all that" He said to us. And lest I cry out that the poor sheep are too stupid to discern truth without me telling them what the Word says, Jesus tells us in John 15, evidently in anticipation of our ministerial egos, that the Holy Spirit would guide us into all truth—not another man.

The word "pastor" is not even in Scripture; the word "pastors" is only used twice. According to Jesus, those in leadership in the kingdom are to be last and not desire to make a name for themselves. And while we are on words in Scripture, the word "layman" is also not in Scripture. Yes, some versions use that word, but the literal translation of that word is "stranger or sojourner." "Layman" is an unbiblical word which should not be applied to anyone who is a believer in Jesus. According to I Peter 2:9, believers in Christ are "a chosen race, a royal priesthood, a holy nation, a people for God's own possession, so that you may proclaim the excellencies of Him who has called you out of darkness into His marvelous light." This is known as the "priesthood of the believer" and means that all in Christ are priests—not just the educated few.

Do not get me wrong—there is a place for ministry and leadership. According to Ephesians 4:11-12 "And He gave some as apostles, and some as prophets, and some as evangelists, and some as pastors and teachers, for the equipping of the saints for the work of ministry, to the building up of the body of Christ." These verses are often labeled "The 5 Fold Ministry"; but a closer look shows us that, again, we have interpreted this wrongly. If you will notice, it is the 5 listed offices who equip the saints (that is you) for the work of the ministry. It is the saints, the "layman", the common man and woman in Christ who is the minister. And as to leadership, I Peter 5 states, "Therefore, I exhort the elders among you, as your fellow elder and witness of the sufferings of Christ, and a partaker also of the glory that is to be revealed, shepherd the flock of God among you, exercising oversight not under compulsion, but voluntarily, according to the will of God; and not for sordid gain, but with eagerness; nor yet as lording it over those allotted to your charge, but proving to be examples to the flock." Jesus said in Matthew 23, "Do not be called leaders; for One is your leader, Christ." In Luke 22, He stated, "But it is not this way with you, but the one who is the greatest among you must become like the youngest, and the leader like the servant." When I am exalting myself or my "position" I am walking in opposition to Christ and His life; and am in agreement with Satan's exaltation of himself. Leaders lead; they do not coerce, manipulate, or shove from behind; they lead.

I am afraid one of the main reasons we do not hear relationship with God and personal meditation stressed from our pulpits is man's lower nature, the desire to "be as the Most High" that exists in our ministers; the desire for others to be dependent on me in their relationship with God rather than dependant on God. It exists in all of us; it is just of a very serious nature when involved in those who, at least in name, are leaders in the body of Christ. We are to be pointing others to a relationship with the Father through Jesus, the Son; not to a pastor, evangelist, or denomination.

As we have already stated, Satan's attacks on God and His kingdom are focused on negating the Word of God to man. One of the most frightening statements in Scripture comes from Mark 4: 18-19, "And others are the ones on whom seed was sown among the thorns; these are the ones who have heard the word, but the worries of the world, and the deceitfulness of riches, and the desires for other things enter in and choke the word, and it becomes unfruitful." Did you really hear that? The Word of God can in fact become unfruitful!!! Jesus tells us that worry, the deceit of riches, and desires—the normal human life—negates the power of God's Word to the point it produces nothing in my life. How? If you will notice, all three of these are forms of meditation. It is meditation on things other than the truth of God's Word that negates its power. Satan and his world system assail us constantly with the demand to meditate on the kingdom of self and its desires. And the main point of the attack is not to provide me with what I want, but to keep me from meditation on God's Word.

With that in mind let us look at another spiritual principle. Jesus stated in Mark 3: 27 "But no one can enter the strong man's house and plunder his property unless he first binds the strong man, and then he will plunder his house." Jesus is speaking here of divided affections. But He then gives the spiritual principle that binding a strong man will allow a thief to plunder his house. But let us consider something about this principle which perhaps you have not asked: If you know about binding a strong man to plunder his house, do you think that Satan may also know that to be a spiritual principle? And if he knows that spiritual principle (especially since it is applied by Jesus to thievery) do you think he might use it against you, and if so, how? Let us consider the armor of God listed in Ephesians 6. Imagine that you are wearing the armor. Now imagine that you are bound with rope while wearing that armor. Being bound will not affect the function of the helmet of salvation, the breastplate of righteousness, or the preparation of the gospel of peace; even the shield of faith will work in a limited way. The one piece of the armor that will not work is the sword of the Spirit—the Word of God. And Satan knows this. And he binds us.

He binds us with our love for the world system, our love for things, accolades, power, control, money, self. He binds us with the world's entertainment, music, books, and philosophies. He binds us with worry, desires, the news of the day, gossip, unforgiveness. He binds us with self-importance, sports, religion—anything that is **not** the Word of God. As stated earlier—this is his main and consistent point of attack—the Word of God. Satan does not care if you have "great" praise and worship (true worshipers are in "Spirit and in truth"—His Word is truth). He does not care if you manifest all the gifts of the Spirit (love is the "more excellent way" spoken of in 1 Corinthians14:31 and love is from the Law). He does not care if you have long and loud prayer services (see Proverbs 28:9 if you don't believe that one). **The Kingdom of God comes from the Word of God and nothing else!!!** It is the Word getting into mankind that Satan fears the most—not doctrine, not faithless prayer, not loud, hollow "worship" producing far more emotion than devotion.

And he binds us with busyness. We see this in the sixth chapter of Acts. The twelve apostles are busy—waiting on tables. I suppose it was a good thing that the leaders were servants, but in verse 2, they state it is not good for them to be doing so. Because in doing so they were "neglecting the Word of God." It is here we see the first deacons appointed and the amazing miracles that happened at their hands. But something very important is hidden. We do see these amazing miracles, but not from the apostles. Instead, we see the church under them explode with power. Stephen, Phillip, Cornelius, the good news goes to the Gentiles, Paul's conversion and life of missions, and the unstoppable spread of Christianity over the entire world—all after the leadership of the early church choose to loose their binding of busyness and instead devote themselves "to prayer and to the ministry of the word." The "twelve apostles of the Christ" die in obscurity; what we know of their deaths only from tradition, only the death of James is recorded in the Bible and that in one sentence. None of their names on the church marquee; they never made it on the bestsellers list or on to a billboard; they never made it to the Vatican. They sought to let the name of Christ be known and their name not be known. They, as leaders, devoted themselves to the Word of God and prayer—and the church, the bride of Christ whom they served—exploded and became unstoppable. They, as leaders, covered the church with prayer and the Word. They, like Christ, sanctified themselves in the Word, and those under them received sanctification. The result from the leaders giving themselves to the Word and prayer was, according to the Bible that the people held the new church in "high esteem" and "multitudes...were constantly being added to their numbers" (Acts 5:13-14). What a far cry from the compromised, religious organization which has lost its taste and is trampled underfoot, distained by men.

I recently heard an interview with a pastor, who when asked why there seem to be a disconnect with what people professed to be as Christians and their ungodly behaviors, responded that his church was growing in numbers and they were very busy. I thought I would be ill. This man was a major player in his denomination, has a large congregation, and as such, influences perhaps tens or hundreds of thousands of lives—and his only response to Christians acting as the world would act was defense of his actions, numbers, and the busyness of "his church." Is it any wonder that Jesus would say that He will vomit the lukewarm out of His mouth?

In John 15:6 Jesus says, "If anyone does not abide in Me, he is thrown away as a branch and dries up; and they gather them, and cast them into the fire and they are burned." This is a poignant description of today's religious church. It abides in its programs and its inflated view of itself and not in Christ. It is dry and lifeless, despite its self created emotional highs, brought on by embracing those who will tickle its ears, agreeing with its pomposity. It gathers itself together in large conclaves, choosing emotional synergy over the true power of the Word of God, putting out intense emotional heat and flame for a time, but in the end, the individual lives are but cold ash, bearing false witness to the false gospel which says "ME" and my feelings and comfort are the central point of life.

Some may protest that they abide in Christ and the above description is false due to that fact. But do we define "abiding in Christ" Biblically? I John 3:24 defines very specifically what abiding in Christ is: "The one who keeps (*tereo*) His commandments abides in Him, and He in him." God will not let us get away with our cheap and false definitions of a pandering God, who is just dying (literally) to let a group of self-seeking, compromised people into the Kingdom of God. If one does not love God's Word, he does not love God—Period.

True leadership is not pushing from behind. Leadership does not manipulate. Repeating: Leaders lead.

And they lead all the time, not just in crisis. In Mark 9 we see the story of the demonized boy who is thrown into seizures. Jesus' disciples cannot cast the demon out, but Jesus can. When asked by His disciples why they could not cast out the demon, Jesus replies, "This kind cannot come out by anything but prayer." What we do not see is Jesus going into a panic, telling everyone that He will be back in a few days after He has prayed. He had already prayed. Leaders lead; leaders lay down their time for God and those under them. Leaders pray before the problem arises—not at the time it appears. Leaders in the church spend time with The Head of the church. Leaders in the church abide in Christ by keeping His commandments, leading others to do the same, non-dependent on the pastor or a denomination.

Make no doubt of it—denominations dominate. They are the masters which tell people what to believe and with whom they may associate. Denominations divide. They rip and tear apart the body of Christ as a ravenous wolf feeding on its stunned, stupified prey.

Carefully consider the following Scripture from John 17:

19 "For their sakes I sanctify Myself, that they themselves also may be sanctified in truth.

20 "I do not ask on behalf of these alone, but for those also who believe in Me through their word;

21 that they may all be one; even as You, Father, are in Me and I in You, that they also may be in Us, so that the world may believe that You sent Me.

22 "The glory which You have given Me I have given to them, that they may be one, just as We are one;

23 I in them and You in Me, that they may be perfected in unity, so that the world may know that You sent Me, and loved them, even as You have loved Me"

Note the phrases in verses 21 and 23, "so that the world may believe that You sent Me" and "so that the world may know that You sent Me." The focus is on the world knowing and believing that the Savior Jesus Christ was sent from God the Father. But it is the small word "so" at the beginning of each phrase which concerns us here. "So" refers to the reason Jesus says the world will believe; that reason is the oneness of those who believe—the unity of the Body of Christ. If you are a denominational leader or a pastor, elder, or deacon, sold out to the company line— jealously guarding your flock (and its money) from the "cult" down the street because they don't believe like you believe in minute trivia; if you are a willing part to the butchery of the body of Christ, watching the robes of the murderers; if you work and travel to spread your doctrines, to make one new proselyte twice the son of hell that you are, you, no, we all are guilty of the body and blood of the Lord, of drinking judgment to himself for not judging the body rightly; judged as guilty for the world's refusal to believe because we have refused to be one in Him.

Here, I must commend you for at least reading this book—you have been humble enough to put up with this tirade. But I also must add here that our egos, our lust for power and control, our fear driven need to "be right" (Do you really believe your Father requires that of you?) will never be changed without exchanging the belief system of organized religion and its self-perpetuating pomposity with the Word of God through meditation—giving yourself to the Word and to prayer; dying to self and numbers, perceived success, and living for Christ and others. The early church leaders gave themselves to the Word of God and prayer—and things have never been the same on planet earth. We do not have a better way. Treating the Body of Christ as a business or institution and doing things man's way must be abandoned and the true ways of God and His kingdom embraced.

Jesus said, "Apart from me you can do nothing." There is much nothing being done, whitewashed with just a quoting His name like a magic incantation. I am afraid that much that has been credited to the church has actually been done in spite of the church. Christ is the true vine—not a church. Christ is the true shepherd—not a pastor or pope. We are to be one in Him—not one in my pet organization.

Then—Jesus said it; it's a promise—then the world will believe.

CHAPTER 16
The Practical Matters

I hope that from reading the previous chapters you have begun to see the fundamental and imperative importance of the Word of God, and the "keeping and observing" (meditating) on it. You cannot and will not obey His Word unless you agree with it. And you will not agree with His Word until it is in your heart. And the Word will not enter your heart except through meditation.

We have seen from Scripture that those who love God keep His commandments; and God has said that is the only way to love Him. We have shown that the promise of the baptism in the Holy Spirit is connected to "keeping" His commandments. It has been shown that abiding in Him and Him abiding in us is directly promised only if we "keep" His Word. Being a disciple is defined by abiding in His Word. Central promises of the New Covenant are relationship with God, dependant upon forgiveness from God, but relationship dependant upon the Law being written in our hearts. The Kingdom of Heaven's growth and genesis is dependant upon the implantation of the Word of God. True, Christian love is defined only by the Law of God. Our love in marriage is to be as Christ's love for the church, sanctifying one another with meditation of the heart on God's Word. We are to be different; a peculiar people. How shall we be so if we have allowed the world's belief system to be the meditations of our hearts and therefore, the behavior of our lives?

But what is Christian meditation and how is it done?

Many Christians react to the very word "meditation" because they associate the word with the world's religions. But one must realize that all things of God are counterfeited by Satan. **All** religions have something right in them. They are designed to confuse mankind and pull him away from our true, loving heavenly Father. If Jesus would state in John 15 that He is the true vine, there must be false vines. Those vines are a tangled and entrapping labyrinth which involves the entire world system, whether secular or religious.

Most religious meditation is based on "emptying" your mind; coming to a point of nothingness and relaxation. It sounds good (all counterfeits do). Mankind is looking for peace. And do not doubt that he can obtain peace through his religion—fleetingly, temporarily. But the fire of war within self still rages. Internally and externally the war continues despite our best efforts. Someone will cross you; something will be demanded of you which you do not wish, but cannot stop; there's that opinion that of someone which we cannot abide: Muslim vs. Christian/Catholic vs. Protestant/ Baptist vs. Episcopal. They must be made to know I am right; their wrongness cannot continue. The war goes on disguised in my smug, self-righteousness, attuned to the constant, eternal mantra from the enemy of mankind—"I am as God." Emptying one's mind is not just a non-lasting patch over the emptiness of one's soul, it also opens one up to further danger from manipulations because the mind has become a vacuum and will naturally pull in all manner of falsehood and filth opposed to the Word and will of God. And while this surrender brings a momentary peace, it is the loss of lasting peace. To empty the mind is to drop its natural defenses, opening it up to suggestions of falsehood which will prove to be disastrous. It is sadly bemusing to watch those violently demanding peace of mankind fighting their unremitting battles for personal peace.

Certainly there is a point of quieting one's mind, but not of emptying it. Christian meditation, as opposed to the emptying of the mind as taught by some, is actually filling your mind and heart with God's Word. Again, the problem with my behaviors is my belief system, what I believe to be true in my heart. Therefore, logically it follows that to change my behaviors I must change my belief system, which is the driving force behind those behaviors. I can resist my belief system; I can, and often do, deny my belief system; but my behaviors, fears, delights, and emotions will eventually tell what I truly hold to be true. Christian meditation is not emptying; it is replacing.

Just as the Christian life is an exchange of my life for the life of Christ within me, so meditation is an exchange of my beliefs (what I hold to be true) with Christ's beliefs (what He holds to be true). We have already established from Scripture that our minds are cluttered with false and wrong beliefs. God's Word is truth. The point of Christian meditation is to replace wrong beliefs, which result in wrong behaviors, with the truth of God's Word. When the belief system in my heart is filled with the truth of God's Word, my behaviors follow the belief system, and the result is Christian behavior.

But as we have already established, a casual reading of God's Word does not produce the results we desire. We forget. We try to obey and cannot. My brain agrees with God's Word, but my behaviors disagree. My heart must be changed; I must get the truth of God's Word from a mental agreement, to a heart belief. And that is through meditation.

Very well, what is Christian meditation?

It is actually not that mysterious or difficult. But it is costly—it costs us our greatest treasure—time. Christian meditation cannot be thought of as a religious duty. It is having a conversation with the God of the universe. And that is the thought one must have in mind. You are going to spend time with someone, someone who loves you, someone who wants to be loved by you; someone who wants to be with you enough to die for you—and did.

But that conversation cannot be reliant upon my just listening to what ever wind may rise in my imagination. Man is far too self-seeking and fickle for that. I must hear God's voice in His Word. "Faith comes from hearing, and hearing by the Word of God." (Romans 10:17) Hearing comes by the Word of God. I learn to hear God's voice by listening to His Word.

And "listening" does not equate to reading. Reading God's Word is a wonderful and fulfilling activity; but taking in small bites of God's Word and thinking about them, allowing them to enter our inner most being is what brings the fruit. Hunger is not overcome by looking at food; one must eat the food. The nutrition which food offers is not gained by looking at a table full of food and then walking away. One must take the time to sit at the table, put the food into the mouth, chew it up, and swallow it. It is only then that digestion takes place and the food which was on the outside becomes part of who I am on the inside. We would never enjoy the taste of an apple if a seed had not been hidden in the ground years before and allowed to grow. Relationships do not spring up overnight. They might start suddenly, but depth and commitment of self comes only through shared words, communication, and experience. I do not read about my wife; I listen to her and experience her. She does not make me a subject of higher learning; she learns me by hearing my words and spending time with me. Why would we think that the Bride of Christ would treat her Groom differently?

Meditation starts with quietness: stopping my thoughts, my activities, my busyness, the pleasing of me—

and quieting my self before God. I find it best to do this early in the morning.

> Psalms 5:3
> In the morning, O Lord, You will hear my voice;
> In the morning I will order my prayer to You and eagerly watch.

> Psalms 143:8
> Let me hear Your lovingkindness in the morning;
> For I trust in You;
> Teach me the way in which I should walk;
> For to You I lift up my soul

Sacrifices and burnt offerings were offered in the morning—including Jesus. And historically those who have practiced such disciplines have found it must be early in the morning, the start of the day, which I give to God; the first part of my day must go to Him or nothing will really go to Him. If one is a parent you know that any hope of quietness is over for the day once even the smallest foot has hit the floor. And so it is with us all. Give of the first of the day to God; rise before the sun; sit alone in the dark of the early morning with the creator of the universe as His Laws change the darkness to light in the world and in your heart.

And I must add here—get out of bed. If you do not rise eagerly to be with your God, your meditation will become sleep. Go to a chair. If you cannot stay awake there, walk. Speak His Word back to Him and to your self. The importance of being awake and spending the quantity of time with God early in the morning cannot be overstated. But now oddly enough, let me tell you the most important place where meditation takes place—your bed.

It is in your bed that you consistently meditate—usually on evil or meaningless activities or worry. Stop right now and evaluate: where do your thoughts go as you are going to sleep? And where do they turn immediately upon waking in the morning? What is your first love? Is it the world and your desires, or the Word of God and fellowship with Him?

Even if you wake and rise quickly and go to sleep quickly, it is imperative that you turn your thoughts to God's Word; that you do not muse and daydream on the things of this world on your bed. As you go to sleep, the thoughts you turn to will dictate your thoughts going to sleep and in sleep. As you wake, the thoughts you turn to will dictate your day. Your meditations in bed order the direction for the coming hours, whether asleep or awake.

But as important as this is, it is a form of more passive meditation. The subject of this chapter is to address active, focused meditation. God's richest blessings are for those who seek His face, who purposefully spend time with Him in His Word and in the Spirit. And it again bears repeating—meditation is not a religious activity; it is a relationship activity. It is listening; not learning. It is "Him-formation"; not information.

And it is with listening we must begin. In I Corinthians 13, the famous "love chapter" of the Bible, there is a list of what love is. And love is first "patient." And the most patient thing I can do toward anyone is listen. If I love God, my first duty is to listen to Him. I must be patient with His Word. Meditation is slow; it does not fit into our desires for instant gratification. The Kingdom of Heaven grows according to the law of sowing and reaping. One sows in one season and reaps in another. Crops do not produce fruit instantly. Fruit requires patience. Most of us would be shocked at how often, forcefully, and favorably Scripture speaks of patience, waiting, perseverance, and endurance. These are the opposite of what I have come to believe as true. And that belief hinders my love of God and others, because love is patient. And the most important place for me to learn patience is in meditation at the feet of God, listening quietly to His Word, rolling it over and over in my mind, engrafting it into my heart.

This concept is so important. All meditations involve some form of repetition. One may be involved in false religions and repeat their mantras over and over attempting to empty one's mind. More common than this with all people is what the Bible calls "vain imaginations," the images I allow my mind to dwell on which are perverse or impossible. I imagine myself in some heroic role, as a great sports hero, saving the maid in distress, finding that relationship/job/car/house which finally fulfilled me, or getting the recognition for which I long and think I deserve. All of these are repetitions in my mind. You see, meditation is not a new concept to you; nor is the patient repetition which it requires. You actually have done these for years. The question is: Will you allow God's Word to be your "mantra"? Have you ever imagined yourself poor in spirit, long-suffering, crucified with Christ, hated by the world, not loving the things of this world, dead to sin? Have you ever, instead of reliving imaginations over and over in your mind, allowed God's Word to repeat over and over in your mind? We have all meditated, and done so often and repetitively. Worry is meditation. Anxiety is meditation. Lack of forgiveness or anger at someone is meditation—repetitive meditation. The repetitive thoughts wash over our minds like running water over a cloth covered with mud. The water changes the appearance and character of the cloth. It washes the cloth of mud, and leaves the cloth soaked with water. It is the same with our minds. Repetitive thoughts remove what is already in my mind and replaces it with the subject of the repetitive thoughts. One may think of it as brainwashing. Normally, brainwashing is thought of in a negative way. But true Christian meditation is what I have been looking for all along—it washes my mind with the washing of "water by the Word," (Eph. 5:26) and replaces wrong beliefs with God's beliefs. And now you have the picture—sitting quietly, patiently at the feet of God, letting His Word slowly change you by the slow, but permanent repetitive washing of your mind.

You see the picture—it is allowing a piece of Scripture to roll over and over in your mind, quietly thinking, stopping, listening. Ask questions. This is a conversation. Repeating passages of Scripture to yourself is listening to God. Please hear that: Repeating passages of Scripture is listening to God!!! But a disciple asks questions of the master. And the Master delights to answer. He may not answer right away; and the answer may come at an odd time. God wants us to learn to hear His voice always. That is one of the points of meditation—to become familiar with the sound of God's voice.

And again, meditation is not Bible study. It may involve study. The Holy Spirit will begin to speak to you and emphasize certain words or concepts. Think on them. Look up words in a Greek or Hebrew Lexicon. Take those concepts and roll them around in your mind, listening for the Holy Spirit to speak to you about them. And while we are talking about concepts and words, do not meditate on the entire passage at one sitting. Meditate on concepts, sentences, words. One does not eat a meal in one bite. The best meals take a long time. Think of it that way. Take a bite, and chew it slowly. You may spend weeks on one or two verses. That is good. Meditation is not about getting to the finish line; it is about the process of relationship with an Eternal Being. That will take, and should take—eternity.

As stated earlier, meditation is not about insights—it is about intimacy. Do not go to meditation with the object of learning more about Scripture or gaining new insights. Go for the purpose of having a conversation with your loving Heavenly Father.

As I stated above, ask questions of your Father. Jesus said that the Holy Spirit would teach us, and He will. What does the passage of Scripture mean to me? Do I do what the passage says? What would this look like in my life? And, most importantly, ask Father to form the concept within me. And use your imagination. Our imaginations are a gift from Father which we use for evil so often. Use this gift for Him and allow the Holy Spirit to speak through your imagination. He will give you pictures of situations, words to use, and His Wisdom and counsel for situations you are and will be facing. He will give you supernatural ideas on how to do things and how to walk wisely. The Holy Spirit is your teacher; not I, not a pastor, evangelist, or rabbi. They may be used by God, but God wants to speak to you. You are part of His royal priesthood, and He desires a walking, talking, living relationship with you; Yes, you.

The only question remaining is, "Will you listen to God?" That is the subject of this book. That is the subject of life. Simply stated, meditation is learning to hear the voice of God. ("Faith comes from hearing, and hearing by the Word of God." Romans 10:17). We learn to hear the voice of God by the Word of God. The Bible speaks of no other way to hear God's voice. Prayer is communication with God, and meditation on God's Word is the path to prayer. If you have struggled with prayer, the answer to that struggle is meditation on the Word of God. Meditation leads directly and naturally into prayer, because meditation is listening to God's voice, and prayer is conversation with God—I am now involved in speaking to God. The Word confronts me with who I am and what I am. And it also confronts me with my inability to change that. And here again is where prayer enters in—my desperate situation. I am a failure at life and must have the power of Father to change me. My cry to Him for that change is prayer. But I will never know the need or believe my need until I have "in humility, received implanted (or "engrafted") the Word which is able to save my soul" (James 1:21). And it is when God's Word is abiding in me I have something to pray—for me, for those around me, for the lost. The best prayers are God's words. He agrees with them.

So, meditation is seeking quietness and aloneness with God. It is receiving His Word as truth. It is repeating God's Word over and over in your mind. It is asking questions of meanings and words. It is sitting quietly at His feet and listening for His voice. It is letting the water of the Word wash over me. It takes time. It will appear foolish. It will sometimes be dry. Satan will bring thoughts of everything in the world to keep you from it. He will tell you it is a waste of time and that you should be busy for the Lord. Meditation is true spiritual warfare. Meditation ("keeping" God's Word) is the first Christian duty; it is relationship with God.

Very well, on what should I meditate? I have a suggestion which will never gain much popularity in today's religious, emotion-ruled, non-offensive church: God's Ten Commandments. The scope of this book is too small to show you that the phrase "Not under law" means exactly the opposite of what the compromised church now teaches. If you read the Bible, you will see that God loves His Law. He holds His Word in higher regard than His name (Psalm 138:2). We argue with the world about posting copies of the Ten Commandments on public walls or engraved rocks outside courthouses, but refuse to put them in our memory or hearts. David said, "Oh how I love Thy law." Jesus said, "If you love me, keep my commandments." Father said, "...showing lovingkindness to all who keep my commandments." The only question, is will I love God the way He has told me to love Him, or will I not love God. Start your memorizing and meditating with Exodus 20:1-17. It is short—just 17 verses; I have seen 5-year-olds memorize it. And your fellowship with God will immediately deepen. That's a promise from The Promise.

That is a good place to start. I would then suggest the Sermon on the Mount (Matthew 5,6,7), the book of James, I Corinthians 13, John 14-17. And listen to your Father. He will have His own suggestions just for you. Throw in some favorite Psalms. God will use them all to bring you into a deep relationship with Him. And don't let this list intimidate you. The Holy Spirit is there to help and you've got eternity. This is not a test; it is a relationship. And God wants you to succeed. Remember Psalm 1, "But his delight is in the law of the Lord, And in His law he meditates day and night. He will be like a tree firmly planted by streams of water, which yields its fruit in its season and its leaf does not wither; and in whatever he does, he prospers." God has promised to prosper you in whatever you do as you meditate day and night on His Law. You cannot help but succeed in whatever you do, if you meditate. But first and foremost, you will find yourself in love with God, and walking and talking with Him in a way that you could never imagine. He is life. He invites you to come, to live, to enjoy Him, and to be enjoyed by Him—eternally.

APPENDIX A
Scriptures on "Keeping" God's Word and Meditation

Genesis 26:
4 "I will multiply your descendants as the stars of heaven, and will give your descendants all these lands; and by your descendants all the nations of the earth shall be blessed;
5 because Abraham obeyed Me and kept My charge, My commandments, My statutes and My laws.

Exodus 15:
26 And He said, "If you will give earnest heed to the voice of the Lord your God, and do what is right in His sight, and give ear to His commandments, and keep all His statutes, I will put none of the diseases on you which I have put on the Egyptians; for I, the Lord, am your healer.

Exodus 16:
28 Then the Lord said to Moses, "How long do you refuse to keep My commandments and My instructions?

Exodus 20:
4 "You shall not make for yourself an idol, or any likeness of what is in heaven above or on the earth beneath or in the water under the earth.
5 "You shall not worship them or serve them; for I, the Lord your God, am a jealous God, visiting the iniquity of the fathers on the children, on the third and the fourth generations of those who hate Me,
6 but showing lovingkindness to thousands, to those who love Me and keep My commandments.

Leviticus 18:
4 'You are to perform My judgments and keep My statutes, to live in accord with them; I am the Lord your God.
5 'So you shall keep My statutes and My judgments, by which a man may live if he does them; I am the Lord.

Leviticus 18:
26 'But as for you, you are to keep My statutes and My judgments and shall not do any of these abominations, neither the native, nor the alien who sojourns among you
27 (for the men of the land who have been before you have done all these abominations, and the land has become defiled);
28 so that the land will not spew you out, should you defile it, as it has spewed out the nation which has been before you.

Leviticus 19:
19 'You are to keep My statutes. You shall not breed together two kinds of your cattle; you shall not sow your field with two kinds of seed, nor wear a garment upon you of two kinds of material mixed together.

Leviticus 19:
37 'You shall thus observe all My statutes and all My ordinances and do them; I am the Lord.'

Leviticus 20:
8 'You shall keep My statutes and practice them; I am the Lord who sanctifies you.

Leviticus 20:
22 'You are therefore to keep all My statutes and all My
ordinances and do them, so that the land to which I am
bringing you to live will not spew you out.

Leviticus 22:
9 'They shall therefore keep My charge, so that they will not
bear sin because of it and die thereby because they profane
it; I am the Lord who sanctifies them.

Leviticus 22:
31 "So you shall keep My commandments, and do them; I
am the Lord.

Leviticus 26:
2 'You shall keep My sabbaths and reverence My
sanctuary; I am the Lord.
3 'If you walk in My statutes and keep My commandments
so as to carry them out,
4 then I shall give you rains in their season, so that the land
will yield its produce and the trees of the field will bear their
fruit.
5 'Indeed, your threshing will last for you until grape
gathering, and grape gathering will last until sowing time.
You will thus eat your food to the full and live securely in
your land.
6 'I shall also grant peace in the land, so that you may lie
down with no one making you tremble. I shall also eliminate
harmful beasts from the land, and no sword will pass through
your land.
7 'But you will chase your enemies and they will fall before
you by the sword;

8 five of you will chase a hundred, and a hundred of you will chase ten thousand, and your enemies will fall before you by the sword.

9 'So I will turn toward you and make you fruitful and multiply you, and I will confirm My covenant with you.

10 'You will eat the old supply and clear out the old because of the new.

11 'Moreover, I will make My dwelling among you, and My soul will not reject you.

12 'I will also walk among you and be your God, and you shall be My people

18 'You shall thus observe My statutes and keep My judgments, so as to carry them out, that you may live securely on the land.

Deuteronomy 4:

2 "You shall not add to the word which I am commanding you, nor take away from it, that you may keep the commandments of the Lord your God which I command you.

Deuteronomy 4:

5 "See, I have taught you statutes and judgments just as the Lord my God commanded me, that you should do thus in the land where you are entering to possess it.

6 "So keep and do them, for that is your wisdom and your understanding in the sight of the peoples who will hear all these statutes and say, 'Surely this great nation is a wise and understanding people.

Deuteronomy 4:

40 "So you shall keep His statutes and His commandments which I am giving you today, that it may go well with you and

with your children after you, and that you may live long on the land which the Lord your God is giving you for all time.

Deuteronomy 5:
1.Then Moses summoned all Israel and said to them: "Hear, O Israel, the statutes and the ordinances which I am speaking today in your hearing, that you may learn them and observe them carefully.

Deuteronomy 5:
7 'You shall have no other gods before Me.
8 'You shall not make for yourself an idol, or any likeness of what is in heaven above or on the earth beneath or in the water under the earth.
9 'You shall not worship them or serve them; for I, the Lord your God, am a jealous God, visiting the iniquity of the fathers on the children, and on the third and the fourth generations of those who hate Me,
10 but showing lovingkindness to thousands, to those who love Me and keep My commandments.

Deuteronomy 5:
29 'Oh that they had such a heart in them, that they would fear Me and keep all My commandments always, that it may be well with them and with their sons forever.

Deuteronomy 5:
32 "So you shall observe to do just as the Lord your God has commanded you; you shall not turn aside to the right or to the left.

Deuteronomy 6:
Now this is the commandment, the statutes and the judgments which the Lord your God has commanded me to teach you, that you might do them in the land where you are going over to possess it,
2 so that you and your son and your grandson might fear the Lord your God, to keep all His statutes and His commandments which I command you, all the days of your life, and that your days may be prolonged.
3 "O Israel, you should listen and be careful to do it, that it may be well with you and that you may multiply greatly, just as the Lord, the God of your fathers, has promised you, in a land flowing with milk and honey.

Deuteronomy 6:
17 "You should diligently keep the commandments of the Lord your God, and His testimonies and His statutes which He has commanded you.

Deuteronomy 6:
25 "It will be righteousness for us if we are careful to observe all this commandment before the Lord our God, just as He commanded us.

Deuteronomy 7:
9 "Know therefore that the Lord your God, He is God, the faithful God, who keeps His covenant and His lovingkindness to a thousandth generation with those who love Him and keep His commandments;
10 but repays those who hate Him to their faces, to destroy them; He will not delay with him who hates Him, He will repay him to his face.

11 "Therefore, you shall keep the commandment and the statutes and the judgments which I am commanding you today, to do them.

12 "Then it shall come about, because you listen to these judgments and keep and do them, that the Lord your God will keep with you His covenant and His lovingkindness which He swore to your forefathers.

Deuteronomy 8:

"All the commandments that I am commanding you today you shall be careful to do, that you may live and multiply, and go in and possess the land which the Lord swore to give to your forefathers.

2 "You shall remember all the way which the Lord your God has led you in the wilderness these forty years, that He might humble you, testing you, to know what was in your heart, whether you would keep His commandments or not.

Deuteronomy 8:

6 "Therefore, you shall keep the commandments of the Lord your God, to walk in His ways and to fear Him.

Deuteronomy 8:

11 "Beware that you do not forget the Lord your God by not keeping His commandments and His ordinances and His statutes which I am commanding you today.

Deuteronomy 10:

12 "Now, Israel, what does the Lord your God require from you, but to fear the Lord your God, to walk in all His ways and love Him, and to serve the Lord your God with all your heart and with all your soul,

13 and to keep the Lord's commandments and His statutes which I am commanding you today for your good.

Deuteronomy 10:
22 "For if you are careful to keep all this commandment which I am commanding you to do, to love the Lord your God, to walk in all His ways and hold fast to Him.

Deuteronomy 10:
32 and you shall be careful to do all the statutes and the judgments which I am setting before you today.

Deuteronomy 12:
"These are the statutes and the judgments which you shall carefully observe in the land which the Lord, the God of your fathers, has given you to possess as long as you live on the earth.

Deuteronomy 12:
28 "Be careful to listen to all these words which I command you, so that it may be well with you and your sons after you forever, for you will be doing what is good and right in the sight of the Lord your God.

Deuteronomy 12:
32 "Whatever I command you, you shall be careful to do; you shall not add to nor take away from it.

Deuteronomy 13:
4 "You shall follow the Lord your God and fear Him; and you shall keep His commandments, listen to His voice, serve Him, and cling to Him.

Deuteronomy 13:
17 "Nothing from that which is put under the ban shall cling to your hand, in order that the Lord may turn from His burning anger and show mercy to you, and have compassion on you and make you increase, just as He has sworn to your fathers,
18 if you will listen to the voice of the Lord your God, keeping all His commandments which I am commanding you today, and doing what is right in the sight of the Lord your God.

Deuteronomy 15:
5 if only you listen obediently to the voice of the Lord your God, to observe carefully all this commandment which I am commanding you today.

Deuteronomy 16:
12 "You shall remember that you were a slave in Egypt, and you shall be careful to observe these statutes.

Deuteronomy 17:
18 "Now it shall come about when he sits on the throne of his kingdom, he shall write for himself a copy of this law on a scroll in the presence of the Levitical priests.
19 "It shall be with him and he shall read it all the days of his life, that he may learn to fear the Lord his God, by carefully observing all the words of this law and these statutes,
20 that his heart may not be lifted up above his countrymen and that he may not turn aside from the commandment, to the right or the left, so that he and his sons may continue long in his kingdom in the midst of Israel.

Deuteronomy 27:
Then Moses and the elders of Israel charged the people,
saying, "Keep all the commandments which I command you
today.

Deuteronomy 28:
9 "The Lord will establish you as a holy people to Himself,
as He swore to you, if you keep the commandments of the
Lord your God and walk in His ways.
10 "So all the peoples of the earth will see that you are
called by the name of the Lord, and they will be afraid of you.

Deuteronomy 28:
13 "The Lord will make you the head and not the tail, and
you only will be above, and you will not be underneath, if you
listen to the commandments of the Lord your God, which I
charge you today, to observe them carefully,
14 and do not turn aside from any of the words which I
command you today, to the right or to the left, to go after
other gods to serve them.

Deuteronomy 28:
15 "But it shall come about, if you do not obey the Lord your
God, to observe to do all His commandments and His
statutes with which I charge you today, that all these curses
will come upon you and overtake you.

Deuteronomy 28:
58 "If you are not careful to observe all the words of this law
which are written in this book, to fear this honored and
awesome name, the Lord your God,

59 then the Lord will bring extraordinary plagues on you and your descendants, even severe and lasting plagues, and miserable and chronic sicknesses.

Deuteronomy 30:
8 "And you shall again obey the Lord, and observe all His commandments which I command you today.
9 "Then the Lord your God will prosper you abundantly in all the work of your hand, in the offspring of your body and in the offspring of your cattle and in the produce of your ground, for the Lord will again rejoice over you for good, just as He rejoiced over your fathers;
10 if you obey the Lord your God to keep His commandments and His statutes which are written in this book of the law, if you turn to the Lord your God with all your heart and soul.
11 "For this commandment which I command you today is not too difficult for you, nor is it out of reach.
12 "It is not in heaven, that you should say, 'Who will go up to heaven for us to get it for us and make us hear it, that we may observe it?'
13 "Nor is it beyond the sea, that you should say, 'Who will cross the sea for us to get it for us and make us hear it, that we may observe it?'
14 "But the word is very near you, in your mouth and in your heart, that you may observe it.
15 "See, I have set before you today life and prosperity, and death and adversity;
16 in that I command you today to love the Lord your God, to walk in His ways and to keep His commandments and His statutes and His judgments, that you may live and multiply, and that the Lord your God may bless you in the land where you are entering to possess it.

17 "But if your heart turns away and you will not obey, but are drawn away and worship other gods and serve them,
18 I declare to you today that you shall surely perish. You will not prolong your days in the land where you are crossing the Jordan to enter and possess it.
19 "I call heaven and earth to witness against you today, that I have set before you life and death, the blessing and the curse. So choose life in order that you may live, you and your descendants,
20 by loving the Lord your God, by obeying His voice, and by holding fast to Him; for this is your life and the length of your days, that you may live in the land which the Lord swore to your fathers, to Abraham, Isaac, and Jacob, to give them."

Deuteronomy 31:
12 "Assemble the people, the men and the women and children and the alien who is in your town, so that they may hear and learn and fear the Lord your God, and be careful to observe all the words of this law.
13 "Their children, who have not known, will hear and learn to fear the Lord your God, as long as you live on the land which you are about to cross the Jordan to possess.

Deuteronomy 32:
46 he said to them, "Take to your heart all the words with which I am warning you today, which you shall command your sons to observe carefully, even all the words of this law.
47 "For it is not an idle word for you; indeed it is your life. And by this word you will prolong your days in the land, which you are about to cross the Jordan to possess.

Joshua 1:

6 "Be strong and courageous, for you shall give this people possession of the land which I swore to their fathers to give them.

7 "Only be strong and very courageous; be careful to do according to all the law which Moses My servant commanded you; do not turn from it to the right or to the left, so that you may have success wherever you go.

8 "This book of the law shall not depart from your mouth, but you shall meditate on it day and night, so that you may be careful to do according to all that is written in it; for then you will make your way prosperous, and then you will have success.

9 "Have I not commanded you? Be strong and courageous! Do not tremble or be dismayed, for the Lord your God is with you wherever you go.

Joshua 22:

5 "Only be very careful to observe the commandment and the law which Moses the servant of the Lord commanded you, to love the Lord your God and walk in all His ways and keep His commandments and hold fast to Him and serve Him with all your heart and with all your soul.

1Samuel 13:

13 Samuel said to Saul, "You have acted foolishly; you have not kept the commandment of the Lord your God, which He commanded you, for now the Lord would have established your kingdom over Israel forever.

14 "But now your kingdom shall not endure. The Lord has sought out for Himself a man after His own heart, and the Lord has appointed him as ruler over His people, because you have not kept what the Lord commanded you.

1Kings 2:
3 "Keep the charge of the Lord your God, to walk in His
ways, to keep His statutes, His commandments, His
ordinances, and His testimonies, according to what is written
in the Law of Moses, that you may succeed in all that you do
and wherever you turn,
4 so that the Lord may carry out His promise which He
spoke concerning me, saying, 'If your sons are careful of
their way, to walk before Me in truth with all their heart and
with all their soul, you shall not lack a man on the throne of
Israel.

1 Kings 2:
43 "Why then have you not kept the oath of the Lord, and
the command which I have laid on you?

1 Kings 3:
14 "If you walk in My ways, keeping My statutes and
commandments, as your father David walked, then I will
prolong your days.

1 Kings 6:
12 "Concerning this house which you are building, if you will
walk in My statutes and execute My ordinances and keep all
My commandments by walking in them, then I will carry out
My word with you which I spoke to David your father.

1 Kings 8:
57 "May the Lord our God be with us, as He was with our
fathers; may He not leave us or forsake us,
58 that He may incline our hearts to Himself, to walk in all
His ways and to keep His commandments and His statutes
and His ordinances, which He commanded our fathers.

59 "And may these words of mine, with which I have made supplication before the Lord, be near to the Lord our God day and night, that He may maintain the cause of His servant and the cause of His people Israel, as each day requires,
60 so that all the peoples of the earth may know that the Lord is God; there is no one else.
61 "Let your heart therefore be wholly devoted to the Lord our God, to walk in His statutes and to keep His commandments, as at this day.

1 Kings 9:
4 "As for you, if you will walk before Me as your father David walked, in integrity of heart and uprightness, doing according to all that I have commanded you and will keep My statutes and My ordinances,
5 then I will establish the throne of your kingdom over Israel forever, just as I promised to your father David, saying, 'You shall not lack a man on the throne of Israel.'
6 "But if you or your sons indeed turn away from following Me, and do not keep My commandments and My statutes which I have set before you, and go and serve other gods and worship them,
7 then I will cut off Israel from the land which I have given them, and the house which I have consecrated for My name, I will cast out of My sight. So Israel will become a proverb and a byword among all peoples.

1 Kings 11:
38 'Then it will be, that if you listen to all that I command you and walk in My ways, and do what is right in My sight by observing My statutes and My commandments, as My servant David did, then I will be with you and build you an

enduring house as I built for David, and I will give Israel to you.

2 Kings 17:
13 Yet the Lord warned Israel and Judah through all His prophets and every seer, saying, "Turn from your evil ways and keep My commandments, My statutes according to all the law which I commanded your fathers, and which I sent to you through My servants the prophets."
14 However, they did not listen, but stiffened their neck like their fathers, who did not believe in the Lord their God.
15 They rejected His statutes and His covenant which He made with their fathers and His warnings with which He warned them. And they followed vanity and became vain, and went after the nations which surrounded them, concerning which the Lord had commanded them not to do like them.

2 Kings 17:
19 Also Judah did not keep the commandments of the Lord their God, but walked in the customs which Israel had introduced.

2 Kings 18:
5 He trusted in the Lord, the God of Israel; so that after him there was none like him among all the kings of Judah, nor among those who were before him.
6 For he clung to the Lord; he did not depart from following Him, but kept His commandments, which the Lord had commanded Moses.

2 Kings 21:
8 "And I will not make the feet of Israel wander anymore from the land which I gave their fathers, if only they will observe to do according to all that I have commanded them, and according to all the law that My servant Moses commanded them.

2 Kings 23:
3 The king stood by the pillar and made a covenant before the Lord, to walk after the Lord, and to keep His commandments and His testimonies and His statutes with all his heart and all his soul, to carry out the words of this covenant that were written in this book. And all the people entered into the covenant.

1 Chronicles 22:
12 "Only the Lord give you discretion and understanding, and give you charge over Israel, so that you may keep the law of the Lord your God.
13 "Then you will prosper, if you are careful to observe the statutes and the ordinances which the Lord commanded Moses concerning Israel. Be strong and courageous, do not fear nor be dismayed.

1 Chronicles 28:
8 "So now, in the sight of all Israel, the assembly of the Lord, and in the hearing of our God, observe and seek after all the commandments of the Lord your God so that you may possess the good land and bequeath it to your sons after you forever.

1 Chronicles 29:
18 "O Lord, the God of Abraham, Isaac and Israel, our fathers, preserve this forever in the intentions of the heart of Your people, and direct their heart to You;
19 "and give to my son Solomon a perfect heart to keep Your commandments, Your testimonies and Your statutes, and to do them all, and to build the temple, for which I have made provision.

2 Chronicles 33:
8 and I will not again remove the foot of Israel from the land which I have appointed for your fathers, if only they will observe to do all that I have commanded them according to all the law, the statutes and the ordinances given through Moses.

2 Chronicles 34:
21 "Go, inquire of the Lord for me and for those who are left in Israel and in Judah, concerning the words of the book which has been found; for great is the wrath of the Lord which is poured out on us because our fathers have not observed the word of the Lord, to do according to all that is written in this book.

2 Chronicles 34:
31 Then the king stood in his place and made a covenant before the Lord to walk after the Lord, and to keep His commandments and His testimonies and His statutes with all his heart and with all his soul, to perform the words of the covenant written in this book.

Nehemiah 1:
5 I said, "I beseech You, O Lord God of heaven, the great
and awesome God, who preserves the covenant and
lovingkindness for those who love Him and keep His
commandments,
6 let Your ear now be attentive and Your eyes open to hear
the prayer of Your servant which I am praying before You
now, day and night, on behalf of the sons of Israel Your
servants, confessing the sins of the sons of Israel which we
have sinned against You; I and my father's house have
sinned.
7 "We have acted very corruptly against You and have not
kept the commandments, nor the statutes, nor the
ordinances which You commanded Your servant Moses.
8 "Remember the word which You commanded Your
servant Moses, saying, 'If you are unfaithful I will scatter you
among the peoples;
9 but if you return to Me and keep My commandments and
do them, though those of you who have been scattered were
in the most remote part of the heavens, I will gather them
from there and will bring them to the place where I have
chosen to cause My name to dwell.

Nehemiah 10:
28 Now the rest of the people, the priests, the Levites, the
gatekeepers, the singers, the temple servants and all those
who had separated themselves from the peoples of the
lands to the law of God, their wives, their sons and their
daughters, all those who had knowledge and understanding,
29 are joining with their kinsmen, their nobles, and are
taking on themselves a curse and an oath to walk in God's
law, which was given through Moses, God's servant, and to

keep and to observe all the commandments of God our Lord, and His ordinances and His statutes.

Psalm 19:
7 The law of the Lord is perfect, restoring the soul;
The testimony of the Lord is sure, making wise the simple.
8 The precepts of the Lord are right, rejoicing the heart;
The commandment of the Lord is pure, enlightening the eyes.
9 The fear of the Lord is clean, enduring forever;
The judgments of the Lord are true; they are righteous altogether.
10 They are more desirable than gold, yes, than much fine gold;
Sweeter also than honey and the drippings of the honeycomb.
11 Moreover, by them Your servant is warned;
In keeping them there is great reward.

Psalm 78:
10 They did not keep the covenant of God
And refused to walk in His law.

Psalm 78:
56 Yet they tempted and rebelled against the Most High God
And did not keep His testimonies.

Psalm 89:
30 "If his sons forsake My law
And do not walk in My judgments,
31 If they violate My statutes
And do not keep My commandments,

32 Then I will punish their transgression with the rod
And their iniquity with stripes.
33 "But I will not break off My lovingkindness from him,
Nor deal falsely in My faithfulness.

Psalm 99:
7 He spoke to them in the pillar of cloud;
They kept His testimonies
And the statute that He gave them.

Psalm 105:
45 So that they might keep His statutes
And observe His laws,
Praise the Lord.

Psalm 119:
4 You have ordained Your precepts,
That we should keep them diligently.
5 Oh that my ways may be established
To keep Your statutes!
6 Then I shall not be ashamed
When I look upon all Your commandments.
7 I shall give thanks to You with uprightness of heart,
When I learn Your righteous judgments.
8 I shall keep Your statutes;

Psalm 119:
9 How can a young man keep his way pure?
By keeping it according to Your word.
10 With all my heart I have sought You;
Do not let me wander from Your commandments.
11 Your word I have treasured in my heart,
That I may not sin against You.

Psalm 119:
17 Deal bountifully with Your servant,
That I may live and keep Your word.

Psalm 119:
34 Give me understanding, that I may observe Your law
And keep it with all my heart.

Psalm 119:
44 So I will keep Your law continually,
Forever and ever.

Psalm 119:
55 O Lord, I remember Your name in the night,
And keep Your law.

Psalm 119:
57 The Lord is my portion;
I have promised to keep Your words.

Psalm 119:
60 I hastened and did not delay
To keep your commandments.

Psalm 119:
63 I am a companion of all those who fear You,
And of those who keep Your precepts.

Psalm 119:
67 Before I was afflicted I went astray,
But now I keep Your word.

Psalm 119:
88 Revive me according to Your lovingkindness,
So that I may keep the testimony of Your mouth.

Psalm 119:
101 I have restrained my feet from every evil way,
That I may keep Your word.

Psalm 119:
106 I have sworn and I will confirm it,
That I will keep Your righteous ordinances.

Psalm 119:
134 Redeem me from the oppression of man,
That I may keep Your precepts.

Psalm 119:
136 My eyes shed streams of water,
Because they do not keep Your law.

Psalm 119:
146 I cried to You; save me
And I shall keep Your testimonies.

Psalm 119:
158 I behold the treacherous and loathe them,
Because they do not keep Your word.

Psalm 119:
167 My soul keeps Your testimonies,
And I love them exceedingly.
168 I keep Your precepts and Your testimonies,
For all my ways are before You.

Psalm 132:
12 "If your sons will keep My covenant
And My testimony which I will teach them,
Their sons also shall sit upon your throne forever."

Proverbs 4:
4 Then he taught me and said to me,
"Let your heart hold fast my words;
Keep my commandments and live.

Proverbs 4:
20 My son, give attention to my words;
Incline your ear to my sayings.
21 Do not let them depart from your sight;
Keep them in the midst of your heart.
22 For they are life to those who find them
And health to all their body.

Proverbs 7:
My son, keep my words
And treasure my commandments within you.
2 Keep my commandments and live,
And my teaching as the apple of your eye.

Proverbs 19:
16 He who keeps the commandment keeps his soul,
But he who is careless of conduct will die.

Proverbs 19:
17 Incline your ear and hear the words of the wise,
And apply your mind to my knowledge;
18 For it will be pleasant if you keep them within you,
That they may be ready on your lips.

19 So that your trust may be in the Lord,

Proverbs 28:
4 Those who forsake the law praise the wicked,
But those who keep the law strive with them.

Proverbs 29:
18 Where there is no vision, the people are unrestrained,
But happy is he who keeps the law.

Ecclesiastes 8:
5 He who keeps a royal command experiences no trouble,
for a wise heart knows the proper time and procedure.

Ecclesiastes 12:
13 The conclusion, when all has been heard, is: fear God
and keep His commandments, because this applies to every
person.
14 For God will bring every act to judgment, everything
which is hidden, whether it is good or evil.

Jeremiah 16:
11 "Then you are to say to them, 'It is because your
forefathers have forsaken Me,' declares the Lord, 'and have
followed other gods and served them and bowed down to
them; but Me they have forsaken and have not kept My law.

Ezekiel 11:
19 "And I will give them one heart, and put a new spirit
within them. And I will take the heart of stone out of their
flesh and give them a heart of flesh,

20 that they may walk in My statutes and keep My ordinances and do them. Then they will be My people, and I shall be their God.

Ezekiel 18:
19 "Yet you say, 'Why should the son not bear the punishment for the father's iniquity?' When the son has practiced justice and righteousness and has observed all My statutes and done them, he shall surely live.

Ezekiel 18:
21 "But if the wicked man turns from all his sins which he has committed and observes all My statutes and practices justice and righteousness, he shall surely live; he shall not die.

Ezekiel 20:
13 "But the house of Israel rebelled against Me in the wilderness. They did not walk in My statutes and they rejected My ordinances, by which, if a man observes them, he will live; and My sabbaths they greatly profaned. Then I resolved to pour out My wrath on them in the wilderness, to annihilate them.

Ezekiel 20:
18 "I said to their children in the wilderness, 'Do not walk in the statutes of your fathers or keep their ordinances or defile yourselves with their idols.
19 'I am the Lord your God; walk in My statutes and keep My ordinances and observe them.

Ezekiel 20:
21 "But the children rebelled against Me; they did not walk in My statutes, nor were they careful to observe My ordinances, by which, if a man observes them, he will live; they profaned My sabbaths. So I resolved to pour out My wrath on them, to accomplish My anger against them in the wilderness.

Ezekiel 36:
27 "I will put My Spirit within you and cause you to walk in My statutes, and you will be careful to observe My ordinances.

Ezekiel 37:
24 "My servant David will be king over them, and they will all have one shepherd; and they will walk in My ordinances and keep My statutes and observe them.

Ezekiel 44:
24 "In a dispute they shall take their stand to judge; they shall judge it according to My ordinances. They shall also keep My laws and My statutes in all My appointed feasts and sanctify My sabbaths.

Daniel 9:
4 I prayed to the Lord my God and confessed and said, "Alas, O Lord, the great and awesome God, who keeps His covenant and lovingkindness for those who love Him and keep His commandments,
5 we have sinned, committed iniquity, acted wickedly and rebelled, even turning aside from Your commandments and ordinances.

Amos:
2 Thus says the Lord,
"For three transgressions of Judah and for four
I will not revoke its punishment,
Because they rejected the law of the Lord
And have not kept His statutes;
Their lies also have led them astray,
Those after which their fathers walked.

TEREO

Matthew 19:
17 And He said to him, "Why are you asking Me about what is good? There is only One who is good; but if you wish to enter into life, keep the commandments.

Matthew 28:
19 "Go therefore and make disciples of all the nations, baptizing them in the name of the Father and the Son and the Holy Spirit,
20 teaching them to observe all that I commanded you; and lo, I am with you always, even to the end of the age.

John 8:
51 "Truly, truly, I say to you, if anyone keeps My word he will never see death.

John 8:
54 Jesus answered, "If I glorify Myself, My glory is nothing; it is My Father who glorifies Me, of whom you say, 'He is our God';

55 and you have not come to know Him, but I know Him; and if I say that I do not know Him, I will be a liar like you, but I do know Him and keep His word.

John 14:
15 "If you love Me, you will keep My commandments.

John 14:
21 "He who has My commandments and keeps them is the one who loves Me; and he who loves Me will be loved by My Father, and I will love him and will disclose Myself to him.

John 14:
23 Jesus answered and said to him, "If anyone loves Me, he will keep My word; and My Father will love him, and We will come to him and make Our abode with him.
24 "He who does not love Me does not keep My words; and the word which you hear is not Mine, but the Father's who sent Me.

John 15:
10 "If you keep My commandments, you will abide in My love; just as I have kept My Father's commandments and abide in His love.

John 15:
20 "Remember the word that I said to you, 'A slave is not greater than his master.' If they persecuted Me, they will also persecute you; if they kept My word, they will keep yours also.

John 17:
6 "I have manifested Your name to the men whom You gave Me out of the world; they were Yours and You gave them to Me, and they have kept Your word.
7 "Now they have come to know that everything You have given Me is from You;
8 for the words which You gave Me I have given to them; and they received them and truly understood that I came forth from You, and they believed that You sent Me.

1Timothy 5
13 I charge you in the presence of God, who gives life to all things, and of Christ Jesus, who testified the good confession before Pontius Pilate,
14 that you keep the commandment without stain or reproach until the appearing of our Lord Jesus Christ,
15 which He will bring about at the proper time—He who is the blessed and only Sovereign, the King of kings and Lord of lords.

1 John 2
3 By this we know that we have come to know Him, if we keep His commandments.
4 The one who says, "I have come to know Him," and does not keep His commandments, is a liar, and the truth is not in him;
5 but whoever keeps His word, in him the love of God has truly been perfected. By this we know that we are in Him:
6 the one who says he abides in Him ought himself to walk in the same manner as He walked.

Revelation 3
8 'I know your deeds. Behold, I have put before you an open door which no one can shut, because you have a little power, and have kept My word, and have not denied My name.

Revelation 3
10 'Because you have kept the word of My perseverance, I also will keep you from the hour of testing, that hour which is about to come upon the whole world, to test those who dwell on the earth.

MEDITATE

Joshua 1:
8 "This book of the law shall not depart from your mouth, but you shall meditate on it day and night, so that you may be careful to do according to all that is written in it; for then you will make your way prosperous, and then you will have success.

Psalm 1:
2 But his delight is in the law of the Lord,
And in His law he meditates day and night.

Psalm 63:
5 My soul is satisfied as with marrow and fatness,
And my mouth offers praises with joyful lips.
6 When I remember You on my bed,
I meditate on You in the night watches.
7 For You have been my help,
And in the shadow of Your wings I sing for joy.

Psalm 77:
12 I will meditate on all Your work
And muse on Your deeds.

Psalm 119:
15 I will meditate on Your precepts
And regard Your ways.
16 I shall delight in Your statutes;
I shall not forget Your word.

Psalm 119:
23 Even though princes sit and talk against me,
Your servant meditates on Your statutes.

Psalm 119:
148 My eyes anticipate the night watches,
That I may meditate on Your word.

Psalm 143:
5 I remember the days of old;
I meditate on all Your doings;
I muse on the work of Your hands.

1 Timothy 4:
15 Take pains with these things; be absorbed in them, so
that your progress will be evident to all.
16 Pay close attention to yourself and to your teaching;
persevere in these things, for as you do this you will ensure
salvation both for yourself and for those who hear you.

MEDITATION

Psalm 19:
14 Let the words of my mouth and the meditation of my heart
Be acceptable in Your sight,
O Lord, my rock and my Redeemer.

Psalm 49:
3 My mouth will speak wisdom,
And the meditation of my heart will be understanding.

Psalm 104:
34 Let my meditation be pleasing to Him;
As for me, I shall be glad in the Lord.

Psalm 119:
97 O how I love Your law!
It is my meditation all the day.
98 Your commandments make me wiser than my enemies,
For they are ever mine.
99 I have more insight than all my teachers,
For Your testimonies are my meditation.
100 I understand more than the aged,
Because I have observed Your precepts.

APPENDIX B
Scriptures Indicating the Present Existence of the Kingdom of Heaven

In Chapter 11 I stated we would give some scriptures regarding the present existence of the Kingdom of Heaven. This is actually a short list, but the purpose of this book is not to get into a theological argument over the Kingdom. I am simply presenting a few of the verses in the Bible which clearly indicate that the Kingdom has already come—not in its fullness I understand, but this understanding of the possession of the Kingdom now changes completely how one responds to God's Word. Note the present tense in many of these verses.

Matthew 3:2 "Repent, for the **KINGDOM** of heaven is at hand."

Matthew 5:3 "Blessed are the poor in spirit, for theirs is the **KINGDOM** of heaven.

Matthew 5:10 "Blessed are those who have been persecuted for the sake of righteousness, for theirs is the **KINGDOM** of heaven.

Matthew 10:7 "And as you go, preach, saying, 'The **KINGDOM** of heaven is at hand.'

Matthew 12:28 "But if I cast out demons by the Spirit of God, then the **KINGDOM** of God has come upon you

Matthew 13:31 He presented another parable to them, saying, "The **KINGDOM** of heaven is like a mustard seed, which a man took and sowed in his field;

Matthew 13:33 He spoke another parable to them, "The **KINGDOM** of heaven is like leaven, which a woman took and hid in three pecks of flour until it was all leavened."

Matthew 13:44 "The **KINGDOM** of heaven is like a treasure hidden in the field, which a man found and hid again; and from joy over it he goes and sells all that he has and buys that field.

Matthew 13: 45 "Again, the **KINGDOM** of heaven is like a merchant seeking fine pearls,

Matthew 13: 47 "Again, the **KINGDOM** of heaven is like a dragnet cast into the sea, and gathering fish of every kind;

Matthew 13: 52 And Jesus said to them, "Therefore every scribe who has become a disciple of the **KINGDOM** of heaven is like a head of a household, who brings out of his treasure things new and old.

Matthew 16: 28 "Truly I say to you, there are some of those who are standing here who will not taste death until they see the Son of Man coming in His **KINGDOM**."

Matthew 20:1 "For the **KINGDOM** of heaven is like a landowner who went out early in the morning to hire laborers for his vineyard"

Mark 1: 14 Now after John had been taken into custody, Jesus came into Galilee, preaching the gospel of God, 15 and saying, "The time is fulfilled, and the **KINGDOM** of God is at hand; repent and believe in the gospel

Mark 4:26 And He was saying, "The **KINGDOM** of God is like a man who casts seed upon the soil;

Mark 9:1 And Jesus was saying to them, "Truly I say to you, there are some of those who are standing here who will not taste death until they see the KINGDOM of God after it has come with power."

Luke 6:20 and turning His gaze toward His disciples, He began to say, "Blessed are you who are poor, for yours is the **KINGDOM** of God

Luke 9: 27 "But I say to you truthfully, there are some of those standing here who will not taste death until they see the **KINGDOM** of God."

Luke 17: 20 Now having been questioned by the Pharisees as to when the **KINGDOM** of God was coming, He answered them and said, "The **KINGDOM** of God is not coming with signs to be observed; 21 nor will they say, 'Look, here it is!' or, 'There it is!' For behold, the **KINGDOM** of God is in your midst.

Luke 18: 16 But Jesus called for them, saying, "Permit the children to come to Me, and do not hinder them, for the **KINGDOM** of God belongs to such as these.

Romans 14: 17 for the kingdom of God is not eating and
drinking, but righteousness and peace and joy in the Holy
Spirit.

Colossians 1: 13 For He rescued us from the domain of
darkness, and transferred us to the KINGDOM of His
beloved Son, (Past tense)

Revelation 1: 9 I, John, your brother and fellow partaker in
the tribulation and KINGDOM and perseverance which are in
Jesus, was on the island called Patmos because of the word
of God and the testimony of Jesus.

Ecclesiastes 12:13
Let us hear the conclusion of
the whole matter: Fear God,
and keep his commandments:
for this is the whole duty of
man.

Alive, Inc. is a non-profit organization whose purpose is to spread the good news of relationship with God. We do so through a number of ways, but primarily through literature, most of which is free of charge for the asking. We even pay the postage. As of this date (July 2011) we have given away over 9 million pieces of literature without charge.

We are not associated with any denomination or group other than those in covenant with God through Yeshua, Messiah.

Our policies are to never ask others for financial support or to share your personal information with anyone.

If you wish to help us in sharing the good news of relationship with God by using or giving away the literature we provide you may order online at

keytorevival.org

Or contact us for other booklets at:
Alive
P. O. Box 747
Burnet, Texas 78611

Name_____
Address_____
City_____ State_____ ZIP_____
Email_____
Phone_____